Vatican II: a Bibliography

compiled by

Charles Dollen

Director, University of San Diego Library

The Scarecrow Press, Inc.
Metuchen, N.J.   1969

Table of Contents

143287

Introduction

"Event of the century" was the summation given the Second Vatican Council by a leader of world Protestantism, Rev. F. Corson. Only time can prove that, of course, but every indication seems to endorse his statement. Modern Christianity has certainly changed its direction and a Second Spring seems to be opening up before us.

The major ideas of Vatican II generated a great deal of literature in the ten years since Pope John XXIII first announced "his" Council. This bibliography was born to support a survey of that literature which appeared in The Priest magazine, May, 1969. It covers the decade 1959-1968 with material available in English. With over 2,500 entries and close to 300 subject headings, it will introduce the student and the scholar to the intellectual ferment of that era.

Some words of thanks are in order: to Fr. Colman Barry, O.S.B., president of St. John's, Collegeville, Minn., who suggested the survey; to Msgr. V.A. Yzermans, editor of The Priest, for encouraging me during the long task; to Mrs. Ellen Curzon, my indefatigable secretary; and to my co-worker, Mr. B. Gene Hunt, who assumed many of my duties when I needed extra time for this project.

My colleagues in the U.S.D. Dept. of Religious Science, Dr. John Portman, chairman, Fr. Joseph McDonnell, Fr. Laurence Dolan and Rabbi Joel Goor made many helpful suggestions which I acknowledge with gratitude. Finally there are the indispensable typists, Ellen Curzon and Irene Gutierrez, to whom many thanks are due.

Abbreviations

Am - American	J - Journal
Assn - Association	Just - Justice
Ave - Ave Maria	Lib - Library
Bene - Benedictine	Liturg - Liturgical
Blkfrs - Blackfriars	Lond - London
Cath - Catholic	Lumen - Lumen Vitae
Choir - Choirmaster	Luth - Lutheran
Dgst - Digest	Q - Quarterly
Eccl - Ecclesiastical	Rec - Record
Educ - Education	Rev - Review
Extensn - Extension	Sch - School
Fam - Family	Sem - Seminary
Fran - Franciscan	Soc - Society
Hist - Historical	Theol - Theology
Hom Past Rev - Homiletic	Tdy - Today
and Pastoral Review	Wrld - World
Intr - International	

VATICAN II: AUTHOR LIST

Abbo, J. , The Constitution on the sacred liturgy and
the code of canon law, Am Ecc Rev 151:361-72,
Dec 1964.   A-1.

Abbo, J. , Vatican II, Priest 18:687-89, Aug 1962   A-2.

Abbo, J. , Vatican II and priests, Priest 20:530-33,
June 1962.   A-3.

Abbo, J. , Vatican II and the Divine Office, Priest
20:348-51, Apr 1964.   A-4.

Abbo, J. , Vatican II; major issues, Priest 20:449-
53, May 1964   A-5.

Abbott, W. , Austria's Cardinal Koenig at the Council,
America 108:671, May 11, 1963.   A-6.

Abbott, W. , Cardinal Doepfner's views, America
108:714-15, May 18, 1963.   A-7.

Abbott, W. , The Council, priests and the laity,
America 107:936-39, Oct 6, 1962.   A-8.

Abbott, W. , A doctrinal decree, Cath Mind 64:27-8,
Jan 1966   A-9.

Abbott, W. , ed Documents of Vatican II 1966 Assn
Press $10.00, $1.45 pb Herder & Herder.   A-10.

Abbott, W. , Future role of bishops, America 110:6,
Jan 4, 1964.   A-11.

Abbott, W. , Twelve Council Fathers 1963 Macmillan
$3.50   A-12.

Abbott, W. , A visit with Cardinal Lienart, America
108:802-3, June 1, 1963.   A-13.

Absent from Vatican II; Bishop Kung Pin-Mei given
life imprisonment by China, America 109;652,
Nov. 23, 1963.   A-14.

Achutegui, P. de, The Second Vatican Council,
    Phillipine Studies 10:517-44, Oct 1962.   A-15.

Act three, Newsweek 64:75-6, Sept 21, 1964.   A-16.

Acta et documenta: series antepraeparatoria;
    description, Clergy Monthly 25:228-30, July 1961. A-17.

Acta et documenta series of the ante-preparatory
    phase, Hom Past Rev 61:1154-55, Sept 1961.   A-18.

Adams, M. , ed Vatican II on Ecumenism 1966
    Scepter pb $1. 50.   A-19.

Advent and the Council: an end and a beginning,
    Ave 102:17, Nov 27, 1965.   A-20.

Aftermath of the Council: summing up of the first
    session, Tablet 216:1268-9, Dec 29, 1962   A-21.

Agagianian, G. , Importance and urgency of missions
    in the post-conciliar period, Christ to the wrld
    12:11-20, Jan 1967.   A-22.

Agenda for the Council, Tablet 216:698, July 21,
    1962.   A-23.

The Agenda for the fourth session, Tablet 219:79,
    Jan 16, 1965.   A-24.

Aggiornamento, Senior Scholastic 87:5, Jan 7, 1966. A-25.

Aggiornamento and world suffering, New blckfrs 47:
    58-60, Nov 1965.   A-26.

Ahern, B. , On divine revelation, Hom Past Rev 66:
    557-65, Apr 1966.   A-27.

Ahern, B. , Report from the Council; schema on
    revelation, Bible Tdy no 14:942:4, Nov 1964.   A-28.

Ahern, B. and Maly, E. , Report from the editors
    at the Council, Bible Tdy no. 3:138-9, Dec 1962. A-29.

Alexander, C. , Christ the light of all nations, Cath
    Mind 63:43-9, Dec 1965.   A-30.

Alexander, C. , Missionary Dimension 1967, Bruce pb
    $2. 95.   10   A-31.

Alfrink, B., An appeal for charity, Jubilee 12:41,
    Mar 1965.   A-32.

Alfrink, B., The Council: moment of expectancy,
    Ave 96:5-10, Oct 6, 1962.   A-33.

Alfrink, B., No deadlock, America 108:729-30,
    May 25, 1963.   A-34.

Alfrink, B., Warns against Council shortcomings:
    the three drawbacks of the first session, Cath
    Mssngr 81:6, May 2, 1963.   A-35.

Alivizatos, H., Calls Greek Council ban historical
    mistake, Cath Mssngr 81:11, Apr 11, 1963.   A-36.

All we need is the word go: Africa and Liturgical
    reform, St Joseph Magazine 64:28-9, Aug 1963.   A-37.

Allchin, A., An Anglican reaction to Vatican II,
    second session, Eastern Churches Q 16:267-74,
    Winter 1964.   A-38.

Allen, W., Has the Council regressed? Past Life
    12:51-2 May 1964.   A-39.

Allen, W., Scripture and tradition, Past Life
    12:55-6, Dec 1964.   A-40.

Allmen, J., Remarks concerning the dogmatic
    constitution of the Church, Lumen Gentium, J. Ecum.
    Studies 4:650-83, Fall 1967.   A-41.

Alphabetical list of members of commissions, Irish
    Eccl Rev 99:51-3, Jan 1963.   A-42.

Alter, K., Pope John's birthday marked by Mass at
    National Shrine, Columbia 41:6-7+, Dec 1961.   A-43.

Alting von Geusau, L., ed Ecumenism and the Roman
    Catholic Church 1966, Newman $3.95.   A-44.

Amato, N. De, The ecumenical-Marian age, Priest
    24:630-3, Aug 1968.   A-45.

American Society of St. Caecilia, Petition to Vatican
Council, Caecilia 90:43-5, Summer 1963.   A-46.
Americans come of age at 3rd Council session, Past
Life 12:2 + , Dec 1964.   A-47.
America's survey of diocesan post-conciliar programs,
America 114:825-7; 115:28-30, 136-8, 343, June 11,
July 9, Aug 6, Sept 24, 1966.   A-48.
Among the missing: Jewish observer, Newsweek
60:80, Aug 13, 1962   A-49.
An end in sight? How the fourth session could be
the last, Tablet 218:430-31, Apr 18, 1964.   A-50.
An end to shame? Christians and anti-semitism,
Commonweal 82:237-8, May 14, 1965.   A-51.
Anderson, J., Don't push the panic button, America
115:655, Nov 19, 1966.   A-52.
Anent communism: the Pope's address at the opening
of the Council, America 107:943, Oct 27, 1962.   A-53.
Angell, P., The Orthodox and the Council, Lamp
61:26, Jan 1963.   A-54.
Angell, P., Report from Rome, Lamp 62:16-17,
Dec 1964.   A-55.
Anglican in St. Peter's: hopes for the reunion of
Christians, Round Table 53:111-17, Mar 1963.   A-56.
Anglican observers for the Fourth Session, Tablet
219:757, July 3, 1965.   A-57.
Anglican observers to the Council, Tablet 216:
677-78, July 14, 1962.   A-58.
Anglo-Saxon chronicles; schema 13, Tablet 218:1220-21,
Oct 31, 1964.   A-59.
Ann Patrick, Sr., The recognition of the person,
No Am Liturg Week 25:179:83 (1964).   A-60.
Announcement of text, Tablet 213:163, Feb 14, 1959.   A-61.

Another view of Vatican II: the shortsighted view of
    C. Stanley Lowell, P.O.A.U. director, Christian
    Cent 82: 1596, Dec 29, 1965.   A-62.
Anti-government Basque priests send protest to
    Vatican Council, Cath Mssngr. 82:8, Jan 23, 1964. A-63.
Antonelli, F., The Constitution on the Sacred
    Liturgy, Doctrine and Life 14:37-8, Jan 1964.   A-64.
App, A., Vatican Council decree on communications
    and the US, Social Just 60:307-10, Jan 1968.   A-65.
Appearance of the Council hall, Cath Sch Jrl 62:61,
    Sept 1962.   A-66.
Appel, R., The two-eyed priest, Am Eccl Rev 115:
    258-62, Oct 1966.   A-67.
Arab pressures on the Council, America 111:505,
    Oct 31, 1964.   A-68.
Arabs and Jews; why there is opposition to De
    Iudaeis, Tablet 218:687-9, June 20, 1964. Reply
    by M. Oesterreibher 895-6, Aug 8, 1964.   A-69.
Arabs and the Council, America 110:589, May 2,
    1964.   A-70.
Aranguren, J., The Council in a secular society,
    Cross Currents 12:199-203, Spring 1962.   A-71.
Armstrong, A., A new look at the mystery of Mary;
    model for the Church, the only perfect Christian,
    St Joseph Magazine 65:7, Dec 1964.   A-72.
Arriba Y Castro, Limits of charity; suggests central
    office be established to coordinate all studies of
    economic problems, America 109:476, Oct 26,
    1963.   A-73.
Arrupe, P., From atheism to analysis, Time 86:70,
    Oct 8, 1965.   A-74.
Arsenev, N., Second Vatican Council's Constitutio

de ecclesia, St Vlad Sem Q 9 - 1:16-25, 1965.   A-75.

Assessing what has been done so far and speculating
on what remains to be done, New Blckfrs 46:662-4,
Sept 1965.   A-76.

Assurance in St. Peter's, Tablet 218:1106, Oct 3,
1964.   A-77.

Atkins, A. , Piers Plowman at Vatican II, Blckfrs
44:516-23, Dec 1963.   A-78.

Aumann, J. , After the Council, Cross & Cr 18:75-7,
Mar 1966.   A-79.

Auman, R. , Left to mind the store, America 109:618,
Nov 16, 1963.   A-80.

Aumann, J. , Schema on religious life, Cross & cr
17:464-5, Dec 1965.   A-81.

Aurucchio, J. , Renewed seminary curriculum, Past
Life 25:25-42, Jan 1967.   A-82.

Austrians and the Council, America 107:392,
June 16, 1962.   A-83.

Autumn session of Central Preparatory Commission,
Tablet 215:1136 Nov 25, 1961.   A-84.

Ayel, Bro V. , Various approaches to the Council;
the catechetical approach, La Sallian Dgst 4:21-23,
Summer 1962.   A-85.

Backs Council draft on the Jews, Christian Cent
81:1078, Sept 2, 1964.   B-1.

Baker, J. , The Council and marriage, Marriage
45:7-13, Sept 1963.   B-2.

Baker, J. , Implications of collegiality, Jurist 24:249-60,
July 1964.   B-3.

Baldwin, L. , Irrelevance of Vatican II, Cath Wrld
201:260-3, July 1965.   B-4.

14

Balic, C., Mariology and ecumenism, Unitas
17:185-95, Fall 1965.   B-5.

Bandas, R., Conservatives and liberals at the
Council, Soc Just 57:118-19, July-Aug 1964.   B-6.

Bandas, R., A misunderstanding still, America
109:128, Aug 10, 1963.   B-7.

Banks, R., Thoughts on Vatican II's decree on the
media of social communication, Hom Past Rev
64:868-70, July 1964.   B-8.

Barauna, W., ed Liturgy of Vatican II 2 vols 1965,
Fran Herald Press $10.50.   B-9.

Barnett, W., Thought for the interim; Evelyn Waugh's
remarks on Vatican II, America 108:440-2,
Mar 30, 1963.   B-10.

Barres, O., It was a missionary Council, Mary Tdy
57:46-8, May-June 1966.   B-11.

Barrett, C., Art and the Council, Month 31:15-21,
Jan 1964.   B-12.

Barth, K., Ad Limina Apostolorum 1968, John Knox,
pb $1.50.   B-13.

Barth, K., Thoughts on the second Vatican Council,
Ecum Rev 15:357-67, July 1963.   B-14.

Barth, M., Salvation from the Jews, J Ecum Studies
1:323-6, Spring 1964.   B-15.

Barth's wisdom on Rome, Christian Cent 80:1019,
Aug 21, 1963.   B-16.

Basetti-Sani, G., For a dialogue between Christians
and Muslims, Muslim Wrld 57:126-37; 186-96,
April-July 1967.   B-17.

Basilica of St Peters during the closing ceremony of
the first session of the Ecumenical Council, Illus
Lond News 241:967, Dec 15, 1962.   B-18.

Basset, B. , Priest in the Piazza 1963, Academy
  Guild $3. 50   B-19.
Battles, F. , Ancient Church historian looks at the
  Second Vatican Council, Hartford Q 5:15-28,
  Autumn 1964.   B-20.
Baum, G. , Birth control and the Council, Common-
  weal 81:280, Nov 20, 1964. Reply: R. W. Crooker,
  81:515-17, Jan 15, 1965.   B-21
Baum, G. , The blossoming of Vatican II, Commonweal
  81:130-32, Oct 23, 1964.   B-22.
Baum, G. , The bishops, the laity and the Second
  Vatican Council; Christian collegiality, Cath Mssngr
  79:5-6, Aug 17, 1961.   B-23.
Baum, G. , Clarification of doctrine as a source of
  renewal, Cath World 196:215-22, Jan 1963.   B-24.
Baum, G. , Communicatio in Sacris in the decree
  on ecumenism, One in Christ 3:417-28, no 4,
  1967.   B-25.
Baum, G. , Conflicts and the Council; questions which
  occupy the hierarchy, Commonweal 76:511-14,
  Sept 21, 1962.   B-26.
Baum, G. , Confrontation in the Council, Commonweal
  79:311-3, Dec 6, 1963.   B-27.
Baum, G. , Constitution on the Church, J Ecum
  Studies 2:1-30, Winter 1965.   B-28.
Baum, G. , Corner has been turned on Church de-
  centralization, Cath Mssngr 81:1, Feb 28, 1963.   B-29.
Baum, G. , The Council culminates evolution in the
  Church, Cath Mssngr 81:8, June 13, 1963.   B-30.
Baum, G. , Council ends, Commonweal 83:402-5,
  Jan 7, 1966.   B-31.
Baum, G. , The Council, the press and ecumenism,

16

Cath J 15:7-8, July 1964.   B-32.

Baum, G., End of the beginning, Commonweal
   77:227-30, Nov 23, 1962.   B-33.

Baum, G., End of the deadlock; the Marian question,
   Commonweal 79:251-3, Nov 22, 1963.   B-34.

Baum, G., End of the session, Commonweal 79:393-6,
   Dec 27, 1963.   B-35.

Baum, G., Final session: off to a good start,
   Commonweal 83:52-5, Oct 15, 1965.   B-36.

Baum, G., Five decrees, Commonweal 83:237-40,
   Nov 26, 1965.   B-37.

Baum, G., From the Council; ecumenism and re-
   newal, J Ecum Studies 1:105-7, Winter 1964.   B-38.

Baum, G., Good beginning: third session, Common-
   weal 81:66-8, Oct 9, 1964.   B-39.

Baum, G., Laity and the Council: the collegiality of
   the Church, Blkfrs 43:59-69, Feb 1962.   B-40.

Baum, G., Mid-point in the session, Commonweal
   81:191-4, Nov 6, 1964.   B-41.

Baum, G., New spirit at the Council, Commonweal
   79:125-9, Oct 25, 1963.   B-42.

Baum, G., Non-Catholic observers impressed by
   Church's confidence in them, Cath Mssngr 81:1,
   Nov 22, 1962.   B-43.

Baum, G., On the modern world: Council discussion
   of schema thirteen and of the jews, Commonweal
   83:117-20, Oct 29, 1965.   B-44.

Baum, G., Peace, priests and the missions,
   Commonweal 83:175-8, Nov 12, 1965.   B-45.

Baum, G., The Pope and the bishops, Commonweal
   79:188-91, Nov 8, 1963.   B-46.

17

Baum, G., Reply (to Hans Kung), America 112:279-80,
  Feb 27, 1965.   B-47.
Baum, G., intr. The Teachings of the Second Vatican
  Council 1966 Newman, $5.75.   B-48.
Baum, G., Theological reflections on the Second
  Vatican Council, Cath Mssngr 81:5, Apr 25, 1963. B-49.
Baum, G., Report from Rome; see every other issue
  of Commonweal, Oct 9, 1964 through Dec 11, 1964. B-50.
Baum, G., Triumph for renewal, Commonweal
  77:434-6, Jan 18, 1963.   B-51.
Baum, G., Triumphs and failures; third session,
  Commonweal 81:377-81, Dec 11, 1964.   B-52.
Baum, G., Turning point at the Council; the debate
  on the sources of revelation schema, Commonweal
  77:334-37, Dec 21, 1962.   B-53.
Baum, G., Vatican II's constitution on revelation:
  history and interpretation, Theol Studies 28: 51-75,
  Mar 1967.   B-54.
Baum, G., What can the Ecumenical Council do in
  regard to the Jewish people? Cath Mssngr 81:5,
  Jan 24, 1963.   B-55.
Be with the Council; Bp Lichtenberger's request for
  prayers, America 107:645-46, Aug 25, 1962.   B-56.
Bea, A., Address to the Foreign Press Club in Rome;
  importance of the Council, Cath Mssngr 8:5,
  May 17, 1962.   B-57.
Bea, A., Church and Mankind 1967, Fran Herald
  Press $6.50.   B-58.
Bea, A., Church and the Jewish People 1966,
  Harper $4.50   B-59.
Bea, A., The Council and Christian unity, Furrow
  13:311-26, June 1962.   B-60.

18

Bea, A., The Council and the Protestants, Month
27:5-14, Jan 1962.   B-61.

Bea, A., The Council and the unity of Christians,
Unitas 14:40-56, Spring 1962.   B-62.

Bea, A., The Council in the Protestant path: agree-
ments and difficulties, Cath Mssngr 79:5, Oct 26,
1962.   B-63.

Bea, A., The decree on ecumenism, Month
34:15-27, July 1965.   B-64.

Bea, A., The decree on ecumenism, Month
33:145-56, Mar 1965.   B-65.

Bea, A., From renewal to unity, Christian Cent
79:1314-15, Oct 31, 1962. Reply: R. C. Stroup
79-1487-88, Dec 5, 1962.   B-66.

Bea, A., Protestants and the Council, Furrow
13:3-15, Jan 1962.   B-67.

Bea, A., Schema on ecumenism, Cath Mssngr
82:12, Apr 23, 1964.   B-68.

Bea, A., A talk with Card Bea, America 107:584-90,
Aug 11, 1962. Cath Dgst 27:103-11, Dec 1962.   B-69.

Bea, A., Urges Council to act charitably toward
Jews, Cath Mssngr 82:5, Oct 15, 1964.   B-70.

Bea., A., Way to Unity after the Council 1966,
Herder & Herder $4.95.   B-71.

Bea, A., Word of God and Mankind 1968 Fran
Herald Press $6.50   B-72.

Beach, B., Vatican II: Bridging the Abyss 1968,
Review & H. $6.95.   B-73.

Beck, C., Christian education, Tablet 1232-3,
Nov 6, 1965.   B-74.

Beck, G., Vatican statement, Times Ed Supp
2632:903, Oct 29, 1965.   B-75.

Beckmann, J. , Roman Catholic missions in the light
of the second Vatican Council, Int Rev Missions
53:83-8, Jan 1964.   B-76.

Behen, J. , One or two Masses? concelebration in
religious houses, Worship 38:656-60, Nov-Dec 1964. B-77.

Behen, J. , Report from Italy; Montini's and
Guzzetti's articles, Worship 35:441, July 1961.   B-78.

Bekes, G. , The Church and its unity: ecumenical
seminar in Strasbourg, Luth Wrld 142:198-204,
1967.   B-79.

Bekkers, W. , Calls for never-ending Council; Cath
Mssngr 83:8, Dec 3, 1964.   B-80.

Belgium's apostle of working youth: concerning Card
Cardijn's speech, America 113:455, Oct 23, 1965.   B-81.

Bennett, J. , The Council and the Jews, Christianity &
Cr 24:134-5, July 6, 1964.   B-82.

Beran, J. , Two interventions of behalf of religious
liberty, Cath Wrld 202:176-7, Dec 1965.   B-83.

Berard, A. , Preparatory reports 1965, Westminister. B-84.

Berard, A. , A program on the Council, Queen's
Work 55:19, Nov 1962.   B-85.

Berchton, S. , Reflections on the use of the sacred
chant according to the Constitution of the Sacred
Liturgy, Caecilia 91:118-20, Fall 1964.   B-86.

Berkouwer, G. , Second Vatican Council 1964,
Erdmans, $5.95.   B-87.

Berkouwer, G. , The Second Vatican Council and the
New Catholicism 1965, Erdmans, $5.95.   B-88.

Bertrams, W. , Papacy, Episcopacy and Collegiality
1964, Newman.   B-89.

Best, E. , Newman's ideas being implemented by
Council, Cath Mssngr 82:6, Aug 13, 1964.   B-90.

Best seats in the house, Time 80:58, Oct 26, 1962.   B-91.

Between the acts: the atmosphere of conciliar Rome
   Tablet 217:391-2, Apr 13, 1963.   B-92.

Between two Councils: 1869-1962, Ave 95:18,
   May 26, 1962.   B-93.

Bevenot, M., The Council's declaration on religious
   freedom, Heythrop 8:405-11, Oct 1967.   B-94.

Bianchi, E., Decree on ecumenism, America 111:776-7,
   Dec 12, 1964.   B-95.

Bianchi, E., John XXIII and American Protestants
   1968, Corpus $6.95.   B-96.

Bianchi, E., Three giant steps, America 111:776-8,
   Dec 12, 1964.   B-97.

Billy, M., Vatican II and the religious, Cord 14:146-52,
   May 1964.   B-98.

Binz, L., Reply (to America: Council's fathers'
   charges) America 110:42-3, Jan 11, 1964.   B-99.

Bird, T., The Orthodox at the Council, Commonweal
   77:148-49, Nov 2, 1962.   B-100.

Birth control; plea that Council re-examine tradi-
   tional teaching, Commonweal 81:216, Nov 13, 1964. B-101.

Bishop denounces Council experts, Christian Cent
   81:724, June 3, 1964.   B-102.

Bishops and the coming Council; Card Koining's
   remarks, Tablet 215:164, Feb 18, 1961.   B-103.

The bishops and the Jews: proposed draft, Ave
   98:13, Nov 23, 1963.   B-104.

Bishops appraise the Council, America 110:141-2,
   Jan 25, 1964.   B-105.

The bishops around the Pope; the Council opens with
   concelebrations, Tablet 218:1049-50, Sept 19, 1964. B-106.

Bishops as pastor, marriage and the role of the
   laity; report of the 6th session of the Cent Prep
   Comm, Cath Mssngr 80:5, Sept 6, 1962.   B-107.
Bishops: Canada; the work of the Council, Cath Mind
   60:57-62, Oct 1962.   B-108.
Bishops' collegiality headed for approval, Cath Mssngr
   81:1, Oct 10, 1963.   B-109.
Bishops differ on conference powers, Christian Cent
   80:1457, Nov 27, 1963.   B-110.
Bishops from East Europe, Tablet 217:1075-6,
   Oct 5, 1963.   B-111.
Bishops from the Church of silence, Tablet 216:970,
   Oct 13, 1962.   B-112.
Bishops: Netherlands; the coming Ecumenical Council;
   pastoral letter, Cath Mind 59:364-80, Aug 1961.   B-113.
Bishops: Netherlands, pastoral on the Council,
   Liturgy 30:101-03, Oct 1961.   B-114.
Bishops: Netherlands, pastoral letter of the hierarchy
   about the Council; East Churches Q 14:62-63,
   Sept 1961.   B-115.
Bishops: Netherlands, pastoral on the Council; Eng
   tr Cath Mssngr 79:506, May 4, 1961.   B-116.
The Bishops of France present the Constitution,
   Worship 38:308-14, May 1964.   B-117.
Bishops: US Decree of Apr 2, 1964 on the use of
   English in the Mass, sacraments, sacramentals
   and Divine Office in the United States in accordance
   with the Constitution on the liturgy of the Second
   Vatican Council, Cath Mssngr 82:5, May 28, 1964.
   Jurist 24:362-5, July 1964, Jurist 24:365-8, July
   1964. Commentaries   B-118.

22

Bishops: US statement on the Ecumenical Council,
Cath Mind 60:52-56, Oct 1962; Cath Mssngr 80:1,
Aug 23, 1962; Unitas 14:210-15, Fall 1962; German tr Herder-K 17:46-8, Oct 1962. Commentaries.   B-119.

Bishops: United States, On the Ecumenical Council
1962, N. C. W. C.   B-120.

Bishops vote rule by divine right, Christian Cent
80:1394, Nov 13, 1963.   B-121.

Bitter end, Newsweek 64:68-9, Nov 30, 1964. B-122.

Blakemore, W. , Catholic and Protestant renewal:
a Protestant viewpoint, Cath Wrld 201:183-8,
June 1965.   B-123.

Blakemore, W. , Protestantism at the Notre Dame
Conference, Christian Cent 83:506-10, Apr 20,
1966.   B-124.

Blanshard, P. , God, Theology and love: the problem
of sex at Vatican II, Encounter 27:51-6, Sept 1966. B-125.

Blanshard, P. , Liberty within the Catholic Church,
Cath Wrld 203:335-40, Sept 1966.   B-126.

Blanshard, P. , Paul Blanshard on Vatican II 1966,
Beacon $5. 95, pb $2. 45.   B-127.

Blehl, V. , The Council: Newman and the problem of
freedom and authority, America 107:950-52,
Oct 27, 1962.   B-128.

Blenkinsopp, J. , Renewal of the religious life, a
return to the Gospel, Tablet 219:1261-2, Nov 13,
1965.   B-129.

Bloesch, D. , The constitution of divine revelation,
J. Ecum. Studies 4:550-1, Summer 1967. B-130.

Bodoni, L. , The new liturgy, challenge and promise,
Jubilee 12:9-11, Jan 1965. (Replies 12:13-15,
July 1965.)   B-131.

Bolder schema on ecumenism is good news, Ave,
99:17, March 28, 1964.   B-132.

Bonds of baptism between Christians stressed by
Card. Bea at reception of Council observers,
Unitas 14:220-21, Fall 1962.   B-133.

Bonds of baptism stronger than all our divisions:
remarks of Card Bea and Dr. Schlink, Cath Mssngr
80:4, Oct 25, 1962.   B-134.

Bonino, J. M. , Vatican II and Latin America,
Christian Cent 81:1616-7, Dec 30, 1964.   B-135.

Books, Christianity & Cr. 22:169, Oct 1, 1962.   B-136.

Borgese, E. M. , Church embraces the future,
Nation 196:23-7, Jan 12, 1963.   B-137.

Borgese, E. M. , Ecumenical Council: empire to
commonwealth, Nation 200:51-5, Jan 18, 1965.   B-138.

Borgese, E. M. , Vatican II: anathema upon war,
Nation, 202:415-21, April 11, 1966.   B-139.

Borgese, E. M. , Vision of a modern Church, Nation
198:46-9, Jan 13, 1964.   B-140.

Bosler, R. , Card. Ruffini's dissent soptlights key
issue on the laity, Cath Mssngr 82:1, Oct 29,
1964.   B-141.

Bosler, R. , Few experts doing most of Council
work, Cath Mssngr 82:1, Nov 19, 1964.   B-142.

Bouyer, Louis, Liturgy Revived 1964, Notre Dame,
pb $1. 25.   B-143.

Boyer, C. , Agreement and disagreement, commentary
on the third session, Unitas 16:304-7, Winter 1964. B-144.

Boyer, C. , The decree on ecumenism of the second
Vatican Council, Unitas 16:243-53, Winter 1964.   B-145.

Boyer, C. , The favorable reception given to the decree
on ecumenism, Unitas 17:137-40, Summer 1965.   B-146.

Boyer, C. The forthcoming Ecumenical Council,
Unitas 12:3-11, Spring 1960.   B-147.

Boyer, C., A Protestant comparison by Lukas
Vischer of the Second Vatican Council with the
World Council of Churches, Unitas 14:89-91,
Summer 1962.   B-148.

Boyer, C., A Protestant view of the coming Ecumenical Council; P. Bourguet's article, Unitas
14:133-35, Summer 1962.   B-149.

Boyer, C., The role of the bishops, Unitas
17:175-85, Fall 1965.   B-150.

Boyer, C., The three unities, Unitas 14:235-8,
Winter 1962.   B-151.

Boyer, C., The world Council meeting at Enugu,
Unitas 17:51-5, Spring 1965.   B-152.

Boyle, A., Cardinal Bea: Apostle of unity, port.,
Columbia 42:6, Sept 1962.   B-153.

Boyle, J.P., Catholic plot against the Catholic Church,
Nat. Revue, 10:489-93, May 21, 1968.   B-154.

Boyle, P., Vatican II has issued 4 constitutions, 9
decrees and 3 declarations. What difference do
these terms have canonically? Priest 22:312-13,
April 1966.   B-155.

Braaten, C.E., Second Vatican Council's Constitution
on the Church, Dialog 4:136-9, Spring 1965.   B-156.

Bradley, R., The post-conciliar situation in Scotland, Clergy R. 52:695-702, Sept 1967.   B-157.

Brady, A., Rome meets the deadline, Italian style,
Information 76:18-22, Dec 1962.   B-158.

Brand, E.L., Vaticanum II on the liturgy, Dialog
4:302-4, Autumn 1965.   B-159.

Bravest schema: number thirteen, Time 84:74,
Oct 30, 1964.   B-160.

Breaking the walls: the curia and the Council,
   Newsweek 62:80, Dec 18, 1963.   B-161.

Breig, J., The Council of humility, Ave 97:21,
   Mar 30, 1963.   B-162.

Breig, J., The Ecumenical Council and convert
   statistics, Ave 100:21, Nov 7, 1964.   B-163.

Breig, J., How about a dialogue on the Vatican
   Council? Ave Maria 95:19, May 19, 1962.   B-164.

Breig, J., Learning from the Council, Ave 98:19,
   Nov 16, 1963.   B-165.

Breig, J., We too have our vote in the Vatican
   Council, Ave 95:19, May 12, 1962.   B-166.

Breviary and missal; hopes for the Council, Commonweal 73:402, Jan 13, 1961.   B-167.

Brickner, B., A rabbi speaks on the Second Vatican
   Council, Cath Mssngr 82:6, Feb 13, 1964.   B-168.

Bridston, K., La Dolce Vita Ecumenica, Christian
   Cent 80:679, May 22, 1963. (Discussion 80:985-6,
   Aug 7, 1963).   B-169.

Bright, L., Vatican II: the internal aggiornamento,
   London Q & H R 192:214-9, July 1967.   B-170.

British reactions to the Council's decree: Board of
   Deputies British Jews, Tablet 219: 1253, Nov 6,
   1965.   B-171.

Brizzolara, B., The coming Vatican Council, St
   Jude 27:19-21, Apr 1962.   B-172.

Broderick, R., Pastoral Guidebook: organizing a
   parish council, Pastoral Life 26:366-8, June 1968. B-173.

Bromiley, G., Papacy: an issue the Vatican Council
   skirted, Protestant View, Church tdy 10:6-9,
   May 18, 1966.   B-174.

26

Brophy, P., Teaching theology in the light of the
liturgy constituion, Irish Eccl Rev 106:227-31,
Oct 1966.   B-175.

Brown, R., Another guide to the Vatican Council,
Ramparts 4:11-14, Dec 1965.   B-176.

Brown, R., Appraisals of Vatican II, session two,
Christianity & 24:164-7, Aug 3, 1964.   B-177.

Brown, R., Apprehensions about the Council, Commonweal 81:441-5, Dec 25, 1964; Discussion 81:530-1,
Jan 22, 1965.   B-178.

Brown, R., Catholicism at the crossroads, Progressive 29:19-21, Sept 1965.   B-179.

Brown, R., Council on the Council, Union Sem   Q
REV 18:49-52, Nov 1962.   B-180.

Brown, R., The Council one year later, Commonweal
85:368-72, Jan 6, 1967.   B-181.

Brown, R., Ecumenical escalation, Commonweal
81:787-90, Mar 19, 1965.   B-182.

Brown, R., Forward steps for Vatican II, Christianity
and Cr 23:174, Oct 14, 1963.   B-183.

Brown, R., Observer in Rome 1964, Doubleday
$4.95.   B-184.

Brown, R., Open letter to the American bishops,
Commonweal 80:411-16, June 26, 1964. (Reply:
P. Hallinan, 80:548, Aug 7, 1964.   B-185.

Brown, R., Protestant assessment: concerning the
decree on instruments of social communication,
Commonweal 79:396-8, Dec 27, 1963.   B-186.

Brown, R., Protestant hopes for the Vatican Council,
Look 28:21-7, Oct 6, 1964.   B-187.

Brown, R., Reformation Sunday in Rome, Commonweal 79:280-83, Nov 29, 1963.   B-188.

27

Brown, R., Religious liberty: fourth and last chance,
J Ecum Studies 2:477-80, Fall 1965.   B-189.

Brown, R., Shadow over the Council, Christianity &
Cr 24:246-7, Dec 14, 1964.   B-190.

Brown, R., Statement on the Jews: a Protestant plea,
J Ecum Studies 2:474-5, Fall 1965.   B-191.

Brown, R., Unfinished agenda of Vatican II, Christianity
& Cr 25:187-90, Sept 20, 1965.   B-192

Brown, R., Using Council Documents, Commonweal
84:254-6, May 20, 1966. (Correction 344, June 10,
1966; Reply 277, June 17, 1966).   B-193.

Brown, R., Vatican II; interview, Way (US) 20:32-7,
June 1964, 14-19, July-Aug 1964.   B-194.

Brown, R., Vatican II: session four? J Ecum Studies
1:514-18, Autumn 1964.   B-195.

Brown, R., Vatican II; session two: an interim report,
Christianity & Cr 23:252-5, Jan 6, 1964.   B-196.

Brown, R., Vatican II: the air is clearing, Christianity
& Cr 24:194-5, Oct 19, 1964.   B-197.

Brown, R., Vatican II: what does the future hold?,
Cath wrld 202:341-7, Mar 1966.   B-198.

Brown, R., Voices of reform and renewal, Christianity
& Cr 24:82, May 11, 1964.   B-199.

Brown, R., What should we expect of the Council?
J Ecum Studies 1:107-8, Winter 1964.   B-200.

Brown, R., What the Pope said, Commonweal
79:165-7, Nov 1, 1963.   B-201.

Buchanan, H., and Brown, B., Speaking out: ecumenical
movement threatens Protestantism, Sat Eve Post
237:10, Oct 24, 1964. (reply: G. Hinson, Christian
Cent 81:1592-95, Dec 23, 1964.   B-202.

Buickens, J., Plans of lessons on the Council,
Lumen 17:648-74, Dec 1962.   B-203.

Bull, G., Vatican Council: the fourth and final session,
Wrld tdy 22:23-7, Jan 1966.   B-204.

Bull, G., Vatican Politics 1966, Oxford Press,
pb $1.70   B-205.

Bumpy road to unity, Newsweek 53:68, May 4, 1959.   B-206.

Burbach, M., The person in the Church, Natl Liturg
Weekly 25:9-19, 1964.   B-207.

Burgess, F., Declaration on religious freedom,
Dialog 5:188-94, Summer 1966.   B-208.

Burghardt, W., Import of ecumenical developments
for theological education, Theol Educ 3:298-307,
Winter 1967.   B-209.

Burns, J., The Council and the layman, Ave 96:18,
Dec 8, 1962.   B-210.

Burns, J.F., Summit in Rome, Ave, 96:18. Nov 17,
1962.   B-211.

Burrett, A., The mystery of the Holy Eucharist,
Liturgy 34:9-15, Jan. 1965.   B-212.

Burton, K., A lament for Catholic women, Sign
44:43, Jan 1965.   B-213.

Burton, K., Women get inside the Council, Sign
44:43, Nov 1964.   B-214.

Busch, W., Lay petitions to Council for vernacular
in the Mass, America 106:107, Oct. 28, 1961.   B-215.

Buswell, C., The Church and the Council, National
Liturgical Weekly 25:24-30, 1964.   B-216.

Buswell, C., Pastors of the Church: the authority of
service, Nation Litur Wk 26:64-70, 1965.   B-217.

Butler, B.C., Consequences, Tablet 221:576-7,
May 27, 1967: 689-91, June 24, 1967; 822-3,

July 29, 1967; 901-2, Aug. 26, 1967. B-218.

Butler, B.C., The constitution on the Church and
Christian reunion, Downside 83:103-13, April 1965. B-219.

Butler, C., The Council phase one: the levels of disagreement, Tablet 217:935-6, Aug 31, 1963. Replies: Sept 7, 1963 and Oct 19, 1963. B-220.

Butler, B., Scripture, tradition and scholarship,
Tablet 219:1316-18, Nov 27, 1965. B-221.

Butler, B., The meaning of renewal, Tablet 221:576-7,
May 27, 1967. B-222.

Butler, B., The seeds of renewal, Tablet 218:1365-6,
Dec 5, 1964. B-223.

Butler, B.C., The Theology of Vatican II 1967,
Darton, 25s. B-224.

Butler, B.C., Thoughts on Theology after Vatican II,
Dublin Review, 516:106-13, Summer 1968. B-225.

Butler, B., The Vatican constitution on the Church,
Clergy R. 51:195-204, March 1966. B-226.

Butler, B., The Vatican Council on divine revelation,
Clergy R. 50:659-70, Sept 1965. B-227.

Butler, C., All of us are theologians, U.S. Cat.
31:21-3, Jan 1966. B-228.

Byrne, V. What to read on the Council, Sign 42:63,
Oct 1962. B-229.

Caird, George, Our Dialogue with Rome 1967, Oxford,
pb $1.75, Peter Smith, $3.75. C-1.

Calderon, C., Council draft on seminaries seen as
basis for reforms, Cath Mssngr 82:9, May 14,
1964. C-2.

Calderone, P., Letter from Rome, Philippine Studies
11:131-41, Jan 1963. C-3.

30

Call of the Council, Commonweal 76:28, April 6,
  1962.   C-4.
Call to the laity; Canadian bishops' statement, Ave.
  95:16, May 19, 1962.   C-5.
Callahan, D., The constitution on the Church and the
  laity, Cath Wrld 202:21-5, Oct 1965.   C-6.
Callahan, D., Problems and possibilities; imbalance
  of lay aspirations and ecclesiastical reality,
  Commonweal 76:439-41, Aug 10, 1962.   C-7.
Camelot, T., Spiritual lessons of the Council, Doctrine
  & Life 13:235-41, May 1963.   C-8.
Camilius, H., Comparative ecclesiology of the docu-
  ments behind the decree on ecumenism, One in
  Christ 3:399-416, # 4, 1967.   C-9.
Campion, D.R., Bishops assess the Council,
  America 108:80-2, Jan 19, 1963.   C-10.
Campion, D., Constitution on the Church, America
  111:777-8, Dec 12, 1964.   C-11.
Campion, D.R., Council jottings, America, 109:110;
  130; 150; 186; 206; 229; 254; 286, July 27 -
  Sept 21, 1963.   C-12.
Campion, D.R., and O'Hanlon, D.J., Council jottings,
  America 109:341-3; 377-8; 409-10; 446-7; 508-10;
  553-5; 626-7; 701-2; 765-6; 791, Sept 28 - Dec 21,
  1963.   C-13.
Campion, D.R., Five views of the Council, an
  assessment of new books, America 110:816-9,
  June 13, 1964.   C-14.
Campion, D.R., Letter from the Council, America
  111:374-5; 406-7; 446-7; 478-9; 512-13; 546-7; 592-3;
  654-5; 736-7, Oct 3 - Dec 5, 1964.   C-15.
Campion, D.R., Loss and gain, America 110:10-14,
  Jan 4, 1964.   C-16.

Campion, D., Remarks on Bishops Cleven, Kuheric,
Spulbech, and Stimpfle in the Council, America
111:593, Nov 14, 1964. (Reply 112:195-6, Feb 6,
1965.)   C-17.

Campion, D.R., Roundup on the Council; annotated
bibliography covering last three years, America
107:847-49, Oct 6, 1962.   C-18.

Campion, D.R., comp., Second Vatican Council 1962,
America $.50   C-19.

Campion, D.R., Third session, America 111:252-4,
Sept 12, 1964.   C-20.

Campion, D.R., Three giant steps, America 111:776-8,
Dec 12, 1964.   C-21.

Can the Council succeed?, America 107:834, Oct 6,
1962.   C-22.

Can we unite?, Cath Wrld 190:209, Jan 1960.   C-23.

Canadian bishops show the way, American 116:573,
April 22, 1967.   C-24.

Canavan, F., Declaration on religious liberty,
America 113:635-6, Nov 20, 1965.   C-25.

Cannon, W.R., Holy Spirit in Vatican II and in the
writings of Wesley, Relig. in Life 37:440-53,
Autumn 1968.   C-26.

Cantwell, W., Congress on Sacred Art and Architecture; Sion Hill, Dublin Furrow 15:653-5, Oct
1964.   C-27.

Caporale, Rock, last Council? America 111:307-9,
Sept 19, 1964.   C-28.

Caporale, Rock, Vatican II: Last of the Councils 1967,
Taplinger Helicon, $4.95.   C-29.

Carberry, J., The Church in the days after Vatican
Council II, Cath Mind 66:7-8, May 1968.   C-30.

Card. Bea at Berne, Tablet 215:936, Sept 30, 1961.   C-31.

Card. Bea in England; views on the Council and unity,
    Tablet 216:758, Aug 11, 1962.   C-32.

Card. Bea on Christian unity and the Council, Tablet
    215:1136-37, Nov 25, 1961.   C-33.

Card. Bea on the coming Council, Tablet 215:290,
    Mar 25, 1961.   C-34.

Card. Bea on the Mystical Body of Christ, Tablet
    216:211, Mar 3, 1962.   C-35.

Card. Bea on the unity of the Church, Tablet 215:1042,
    Oct 28, 1961.   C-36.

Card. Bea sees coming Council facilitating the way to
    unity, Unitas 13:303-05, Winter 1961.   C-37.

Cardinal in charge, Newsweek 55:67, June 20, 1960.   C-38.

Card. Konig confers with Grand Sheikh; Hassan
    Mamoun, Cath Mssngr 83:9, Dec 24, 1964.   C-39.

Card. Leger's problem, America 108:63, Jan 19,
    1962.   C-40.

Cardinal Ottaviani's secret, Month 36:291-2,
    Dec 1966.   C-41.

Cardinal Suenens on the Council; summary of Paris
    press conference, Tablet 217:350, Mar 30, 1963.   C-42.

Cardinal Tardini did not oppose Council; diary, Cath
    Mssngr 82:6, July 31, 1964.   C-43.

Card. Wyszynski sought lay participation in Council,
    Cath Mssngr 81:1, May 9, 1963.   C-44.

Card. Wyszynski under fire, Tablet 217:851, Aug 3,
    1963.   C-45.

Cardinale, H.E., Religious tolerance, freedom and
    inter-group relations in the light of Vatican II,
    Council of Christians and Jews, 25 p. 1966.   C-46.

Cardinale, H. , Religious tolerance, freedom and inter-
group relations in the light of the second Vatican
Council, Dublin R. 240:309-28, Winter 1967.   C-47.

Cardinals divide, America 110:532, April 18, 1964.   C-48.

Cardinals' ideas on religious life opposed by Bishop's
organization; Bishops' Secretarial Committee, Cath
Mssngr 83:19, Dec 17, 1964.   C-49.

The Cardinals' letter of protest to the Pope; schema
changes on Jews and religious liberty, Tablet
218:1210-11, Oct 24, 1964.   C-50.

Cardinal's setback, Time 80:65, Nov 23, 1962.   C-51.

Cargas, H. , Vatican II in recent books; Direction
10:10-12, Nov 1963.   C-52.

Carr, A. , Obliged to prime? members of religious
orders, Homiletic Pastoral R. 64:616-17, April
1964.   C-53.

Carrillo de Albornoz, A. F. , Ecumenical and world
signifigance of the Vatican declaration on reglious
liberty, Ecum. Rev. 18:58-84, Jan 1966.   C-54.

Carrillo de Albornoz, A. F. , Ecumenical perspectives
of the Vatican declaration on religious liberty, J.
Ch. & State 8:445-56, Autumn 1966.   C-55.

Carrillo de Albornoz, Angel F. Religious Liberty
1967, Sheed, $5. 00.   C-56.

Carrillo de Albornoz, A. F. , Religious liberty and the
second Vatican Council, Ecem. Rev. 16:395-405,
July 1964.   C-57.

Carroll, E. , Council not de-emphasizing Mary; sees
her role as model of Church, Cath Mssngr 82:1,
May 7, 1964.   C-58.

Carroll, E. , The faith of Mary, Our Lady Dgst.
20:215-6, Jan - Feb 1966.   C-59.

Carroll, E., Mary and Vatican II, Scapular 23:24-6,
July - Aug 1964.   C-60.

Carroll, E., Mary in the conciliar age, Our Lady
Dgst. 19:91-8, Aug - Sept 1964.   C-61.

Carroll, E., Our Lady and Vatican II, Cross & Cr.
18:277-88, Sept 1966.   C-62.

Carroll, E., Protestant reaction to the role of Mary
in Vatican II, Am Ecc Review 154:289-301,
May 1966.   C-63.

Carter, G.E., Conciliar Rome, America 112:418-25,
March 27, 1965.   C-64.

Carter, G., The Council and modern catechetics,
Cath Educator 35:174-6, Oct 1964.   C-65.

Carter, G.E., Head and heart: catechisms with a
modern accent, America 109:40-3, July 13, 1963.   C-66.

Cartus, F.E., Vatican Council ends: reform on bor-
rowed time, Harper 231:100-3, Sept 11, 1965.
(Reply: America 113, inside cover, Sept 11, 1965.) C-67.

Cartus, F., Vatican II and the Jews, Commentary
39:31-2, June 1965.   C-68.

Casey, G., Same always, please; E. Waugh's hopes
for the Council, Commonweal 77:487-9, Feb 1,
1963.   C-69.

Casey, T., Perfectae caritaties: the sociological chal-
lenges, Cross & Cr. 19:146-54, June 1967.   C-70.

Casserly, J., The Council: a challenge, Cath Lib W.
39:17-21, Sept 1967.   C-71.

Casserly, J. J., The Ecumenical Council, where it
stands today, Ave Maria 93:5-7, April 1, 1961.   C-72

Catalans speak for religious liberty; petition to Spanish
Council father, Tablet 218:1448, Dec 19, 1964.   C-73.

Catching up; need to keep informed, America
109;92, July 27, 1963.   C-74.

Catholic Europe after Vatican II, America 118:67,
Jan 20, 1968.   C-75.

Catholic-Jewish meeting urges separate schema on
Jews, Cath Journal 15:1, July 1964.   C-76.

Catholic ecumenism; the final session of the Central
Prep. Committee, Tablet 216:615, June 30, 1962.   C-77.

Catholic Press at the Council; an opportunity to serve
the Church, America 106:676, Feb 24, 1962.   C-78.

Catholic publications hope for Council's strong statement on the Jews, US Catholic 30:62, Sept 1964.   C-79.

The Catholic Reporter, The Layman and the Council
1965, Templegate, $3.95.   C-80.

Catholic press at the Council, America 106:676,
Feb 24, 1962.   C-81.

Catholic summit; lucky third time, Economist,
212:1006, Sept 12, 1964.   C-82.

Catholic University of America, Workshop on Vatican
Council II 1967, Catholic U., pb. $2.95.   C-83.

Catholic world Council delayed two years, Christian
Cent 76:189, Feb 18, 1959.   C-84.

Catholicism, reaction and obedience; end-of-session
reflections, Tablet 218:1338-40, Nov 28, 1964.   C-85.

Catholics and the rest; coexistence, Economist,
213:23-4, Oct 3, 1964.   C-86.

Catholics hit Vatican II : conversions decline in
Britain, Christian Cent 81:540, April 29, 1964.   C-87.

Cavanagh, J., Bishop discusses psychiatric care of
priests at Council, Guild Cath. Psych. 12:44-7,
Jan 1965.   C-88.

Celibacy and the Council, Tablet 221:713-4, July 1,
1967.   C-89.

Central commission for the General Council,
Tablet 214:612, June 25, 1960.   C-90.
Central Commission on liturgy, missions, communi-
cations, Tablet 216:339, April 7, 1962.   C-91.
The Central Preparatory Commission and sexual
morality, Tablet 216:459, May 12, 1962.   C-92.
The Central Preparatory Commission: here is how
the Church prepares for the Council, Cath
Mssngr 80:5, Feb 8, 1962.   C-93.
Central Preparatory Commission's fourth session,
Tablet 216:211, March 3, 1962.   C-94.
Central Preparatory Commission's third plenary
session, Cath Mssngr 80:5 , Feb 15, 1962.   C-95.
Chabas, P., and Luepsen, F., European reaction
to the Vatican Council, Christian Cent 80:207-9,
Feb 13, 1969.   C-96.
Chandran, J.R., Second Vatican Council: a comment
from Asia, Ecum Rev 15:385-90, July 1963.   C-97.
Change of direction, Tablet 219:875-6, Aug 7, 1965.   C-98.
Chatham, J., Toward a theology of race relations,
Cath Mind 65:48-54, March 1967.   C-99.
Chenu, M., Les signes des temps: The Church in
the Modern world, N.R.T. 87:29-38, Jan 1965.   C-100.
Cherian, C., The Council discusses the Bible, Clergy
Monthly 28:424-8, Dec 1964.   C-101.
Christ in our midst: the liturgy constitution, special
issue, Furrow 15:267-344, May 1964.   C-102.
Christian Brothers episcopal alumni at Vatican
Council II, La Sallian Digt. 6:18-21, Fall 1963.   C-103.
Christian in the world: drafting of a final conciliar
text on the Church in the modern world, America
112:350 March 13, 1965.   C-104.

Christian marriage; appeal by laity to Pope and
    bishops on birth control, Tablet 218:1212-13,
    Oct 24, 1964.   C-105.

Church and population growth, Ave. 98:17, Oct 19,
    1963.   C-106.

The Church and religious liberty, America 113:393-4,
    Oct 9, 1965.   C-107.

The Church and war, America 114:7-8, Jan 1, 1966.   C-108.

The Church and the bomb, World View, 7:4-15,
    Dec 1964.   C-109.

The Church and the Council, Commonweal 77:83-84,
    Oct 19, 1962.   C-110.

The Church and the world, Sign 44:37, Dec 1964.   C-111.

The Church at worship and in the world; 5th session
    of the Preparatory Commission, Cath Mssngr
    80:5-6, Aug 9, 1962.   C-112.

The Church in Council, Dominicana 47:105-78,
    Summer 1962.   C-113.

The Church in the modern world, Sign 45:33, Feb
    1966.   C-114.

The Church, national and universal; the Council and
    toleration, Tablet 216:851-52, Sept 15, 1962.   C-115.

Church of Ireland, Prayer for the Council, Furrow
    13:569, Oct 1962.   C-116.

The Church Today 1968, Newman, $10.00.   C-117.

The Church's catholicity, America 111:372, Oct 3,
    1964.   C-118.

Cirada Lachiondo, J., Sacramentality of episcopacy
    accepted by Council Fathers, Cath Mssngr 81:8,
    Nov 7, 1963.   C-119.

The City and the world; a digest of Catholic opinion,
    View 26:7-10, June 1962.   C-120.

Clancy, John Gregory, Pope John XXIII: an invitation
    to hope 1967, Simon and Schuster, pb. $.95.   C-121.
Clark, A., The training of priests, Tablet 219:1290-1,
    Nov 21, 1965.   C-122.
Clark, E., Pope Paul VI issues a decree on communi-
    cations media, Cath Sch Journal 64:62, April
    1964.   C-123.
A clear statement on the Jews, Sign 44:33-4, Aug
    1964.   C-124.
Clifton, C., The relationship between the religious
    community and the people of God, Natl Liturg Week
    25:173-78, 1964.   C-125.
Closed and/or open; liberal and conservative wrong
    terms to label Council Fathers, America 109:484-6,
    Oct 26, 1963.   C-126.
Cochrane, A.C., Deepening the dialogue, Christian
    Cent 81:1111, Sept 9, 1964.   C-127.
Cochrane, E., Failure in Florence, Commonweal
    85:197-9, Nov 18, 1966.   C-128.
Cogley, J., After the Council, Critic 24:51-7, April-
    May 1966.   C-129.
Cogley, J., Collegiality, Cath Mssngr 82:1, Oct 1,
    1964.   C-130.
Cogley, J., Conciliar Rome: laymen at the Council,
    America 112:420-2, March 27, 1965.   C-131.
Cogley, J., Council session termed magnificent
    success, Cath Mssngr 83:1, Dec 3, 1964.   C-132.
Cogley, J., Grounds for hope, Commonweal 79:398-400,
    Dec 27, 1963.   C-133.
Cogley, J., The Jews, Cath Mssngr 82:1, Oct 8,
    1964.   C-134.
Cogley, J., Laymen rediscovered, Commonweal 79:253-5,
    Nov 22, 1963.   C-135.

Cogley, J., Pope Paul walks lonely road between
liberals and conservatives, Cath Mssngr 83:10,
Dec 3, 1964.   C-136.

Cogley, J., Roman diary: impressions of the second
session, America 111:348-51, Sept 26, 1964.   C-137.

Cogley, J., Schema 13, Cath Mssngr 82:1-2, Oct 29,
1964.   C-138.

Cogley, J., The search for freedom, Commonweal
79:301-4, Dec 6, 1963.   C-139.

Cogley, J., Vatican II re-educates the American
bishops, N.Y. Times Magazine p. 35, Nov 22,
1964.   C-140.

Colainni, J., Mischief of 1417: the Council of Constance,
Ramparts 4:20-2, Oct 1965.   C-141.

Cole, M., From Council assembly to parish hall;
Extension 58:22-3, May 1964.   C-142.

Cole, P., God and the foreign press, Columbia
43:20-2, Nov 1963.   C-143.

Cole, W., Mary at the Council and reunion, Marian
Library Studies no. 101-2:1-17, Oct-Nov 1963.   C-144.

The coming Council; Cardinal Bea's Appointment,
Tablet 214:559, June 11, 1960.   C-145.

The coming Council; hopes, expectations and suggestions
of the laity; letters, Cath Mssngr 79:7, July 27,
1961.   C-146.

Comments of the Council fathers on Schema 13,
Guild C. Psych. 12:47-51, Jan 1965.   C-147.

Commissions of the Council; list, Tablet 216:1026-27,
Oct 27, 1962.   C-148.

The communications schema should be buried, Christian
Cent 81:227, Feb 19, 1964.   C-149.

Communists and the Council, America 107:367,
June 9, 1962.   C-150.

Conciliar breakthrough; the norms for work during
the recess, America 107:1266-7, Dec 29, 1962.   C-151.

The Conciliar constitution De Ecclesia, symposium,
Unitas 17:175-216, Fall 1965.   C-152.

Conciliar counterpoint; collegiality and the diaconate,
Tablet, 217:113-14, Oct 19, 1963.   C-153.

The conciliar mind, Tablet 218:1336-7, Nov 28, 1964.   C-154.

Concrete lines of action, Magnificat 113:29-31,
Sept 1964.   C-155.

Condemnation of deicide charge dropped: Ritter, Cath
Mssngr 82:3, Sept 3, 1964.   C-156.

Confraternity of Christian Doctrine, Vatican II and
Renewal through CCD 1967, St. Anthony Guild Press,
pb. $4.50.   C-157.

Congar, Yves, ed, Council Speeches of Vatican II
1964, Sheed, pb $1.50.   C-158.

Congar, Y. M. , The Council, the Church, and the
others, Cross Currents 11:241-54, Summer 1961.   C-159.

Congar, Y. , Ecumenism at the Council session,
Clergy Monthly 27:70-1, March 1963.   C-160.

Congar, Y. , Perspectives for the Council, America
105:394-98, June 3, 1961.   C-161.

Congar, Yves, Report from Rome II 1964, Palm,
pb. $.95.   C-162.

Congar, Y. , Seeing the Church: a Conciliar topic;
April, 1963, Doctrine & Life 13:507-18, Oct 1963.   C-163.

Congar, Y. , Theology in the Council, Am. Ecc. Review
155:217-30, Oct 1966.   C-164.

Congress of Rites: instruction for the proper implementation of the Constitution on the Sacred Liturgy,
Eng. Tr. Cath Mssngr 82:5-6, Oct 29, 1964, and
5-6, Nov 5, 1964.   C-165.

Conley, W. H. , The Council and the Teacher, Cath. Sch.
Journal, 66:4, Jan 1966.   C-166.

Connare, W. , Faith and religious liberty, Dominicans
53:6-18, Spring 1968.   C-167.

Connell, F. , The constitution on the Church, Am.
Ecc. Review 152:89-99, Feb 1965.   C-168.

Connell, F. , The omission of deicide, Am. Ecc.
Review 154:205-6, March 1966.   C-169.

Connelly, J. , The Liturgical Constitution and the
Society of St. Gregory, Liturgy 33:91-3, Oct 1964. C-170.

Conscience at the Council, America 109:204, Aug 31,
1963.   C-171.

Consolata, Sr. , Concerning virgins, New Blckfrs.
47:525-31, July 1966.   C-172.

Constancy and committment: historical perspectives
at the Council, Tablet 219:1145-7, Oct 16, 1965.   C-173.

Constitution on divine revelation, a symposium, Bible
Today 35:2418-53, March 1968.   C-174.

The constitution on the Eastern Churches, Tablet
218:1356, Nov 28, 1964.   C-175.

The constitution on the liturgy, special issue: Doctrine
and Life 14:63-157, Feb 1964.   C-176.

The constitution on the liturgy, symposium, Furrow
15:85-96, Feb 1964.   C-177.

Constitutions and individual documents available in
pamphlet form from N. C. W. C. , Paulist Press and
St. Paul Editions

      Constitution on the Sacred Liturgy
        Sacrosanctum Concilium
      Declaration on Christian Education
        Gravissimum Educationis
      Declaration on Religious Freedom
        Dignitatis Humanae
      Declaration on the relationship of the Church

to Non-Christian Religious
  Nostrae Aetate
Decree on Eastern Catholic Churches
  Orientalium Ecclesiarum
Decree on Ecumenism
  Unitatis Redintegratio
Decree on Priestly Formation
  Optatam Totius
Decree on the Apostolate of the Laity
  Apostolicam Actuositatem
Decree on the Appropriate Renewal of Religious Life
  Perfectae Caritatis
Decree on the Church's Missionary Activity
  Ad Gentes
Decree on the Instruments of Social Communication
  Inter Mirifica
Decree on the Ministry and Life of Priests
  Presbyterorum Ordinis
Decree on the Pastoral Office of Bishops in the Church
  Christus Dominus
Dogmatic Constitution on Divine Revelation
  Dei Verbum
Dogmatic Constitution on the Church
  Lumen Gentium
Pastoral Constitution on the Church
  Gaudium et Spes
Ad Gentes - Missions - Decree
Apostolicam Actuositatem - Laity - Decree
Christus Dominus - Bishops - Decree
Dei Verbum - Revelation - Dogmatic Constitution
Dignitatis Humanae - Religious Freedom - Declaration
Gaudium et Spes - Church - Pastoral Constitution
Gravissimum Educationis - Education - Declaration
Inter Mirifica - Communication - Decree
Lumen Gentium - Church - Dogmatic Constitution
Nostra Aetate - Non-Christians - Declaration
Optatam Totius - Seminaries - Decree
Orientalium Ecclesiarum - Eastern Church- Decree
Perfectae Caritatis - Religious Life - Decree
Presbyterorum Ordinis - Priests - Decree
Sacrosanctum Concilium - Liturgy - Constitution
Unitatis Redintegratio - Ecumenism - Decree. C-178.

Controversy on a text, America 111:287, Sept 19, 1964. C-179.

Conway, J., Commentary on the Second Vatican

Council's Constitution on the Church, Cath Mssngr
83:9, Dec 17, 1964.   C-180.

Conway, J. D. , Each of us must prepare for the
Council, Cath Mssngr 80:7-8, June 21, 1962.   C-181.

Cooke, B. J. , The teacher's task of helping to attain
the goals of the Council, Society of Cath. Coll.
Teachers of Sacred Doc. Proceedings 8:7-13 1962.   C-182.

Cooke, B. J. , Vatican Council and the ecumenical
vision, Religious Education, 57:290-3, July 1962.   C-183.

Coordinating commission for Council studies new draft
of revelation schema, Cath Mssngr 81:1, April 4,
1963.   C-184.

Coote, N. , Council books, Furrow suppl # 3; 2:2-13,
Winter 1967.   C-185.

Coptic view of the Council, Tablet 216:1284, Dec 29,
1962.   C-186.

Cornelis, J. , An ecumenical evaluation of the second
session of Vatican Council II, Unitas 16:6-15,
Spring 1964.   C-187.

Cornelis, J. , The ecumenical import of the new
constitution on the liturgy, Unitas 16:171-86,
Fall 1964.   C-188.

Cornelis, J. , The general council: the hope of unity,
Unitas 11:85-94, Summer 1959.   C-189.

Cornelis, K. , The Council in perspective, Cath
Mind 60:4-11, Sept 1962.   C-190.

Corson, F. , The Council: "event of the century,"
Unitas 16:314, Winter 1964.   C-191.

Corson, F. , Unity in our times, Cath Dgst 29:35-8,
Mar 1965.   C-192.

Coulson, J. , From Dollinger to Vatican II: a century
too soon? Commonweal 79:400-3, Dec 27, 1963.   C-193.

44

The Council, Jubilee 12:20-6, Nov 1965; 13:6,
Jan 1966.   C-194.

The Coucil: a third session, Tablet 217:995, Sept 14,
1963.   C-195.

The Council adjourns, America 111:734, Dec 5, 1964.   C-196.

Council agenda: views and suggestions of German-
speaking people, Tablet 215:1250-1, Dec 30, 1960.   C-197.

The Council and anti-Semitism, Commonweal
80:407-8, June 26, 1964; reply 547-8, Aug 7.   C-198.

The Council and Christian growth: symposium on Lumen
Gentium, Lumen 20:579-702, Dec 1965.   C-199.

The Council and colleges, America 107:928, Oct 20,
1962.   C-200.

Council and liberty, America 110:335, Mar 14, 1964.   C-201.

The Council and liturgical reform, Liturgy 31:50-1,
April 1962.   C-202.

The Council and liturgy: Central Commission statement, Liturgy 31:75, July 1962.   C-203.

Council and liturgy: first matter for study, America
107:977, Nov 3, 1962.   C-204.

The Council and politics: ratifying the papal socio-
political teachings, America 106:847-48, March 31,
1962.   C-205.

The Coucil and the bomb, Tablet 218:712-13, June 27,
1964; replies 756-7, July 4; 785-6, July 11; 812-13,
July 18.   C-206.

The Council and the churches, Month 27:35-8, Jan
1962.   C-207.

The Council and the colored world: need for guidance
on the problem of racism, Interracial Rev 36:53,
March 1963.   C-208.

The Council and the future, Commonweal 79:27, Oct 4,
1963.   C-209.

45

The Council and the Jews, America 110:842-3,
  June 20, 1964; replies 111:1-2, July 4.   C-210.
The Council and the Jews, Cath Mssngr 82:10,
  June 18, 1964.   C-211.
The Council and the mission apostolate, Shield
  42:24-5, Nov 1962.   C-212.
Council and the missions, Tablet 216:979-80,
  Oct 20, 1962.   C-213.
Council and the press: forebodings of poor press
  relations, Cath Mssngr 80:10, Sept 6, 1962.   C-214.
Council and the press: neither rubber stamps nor
  Machiavelles, Tablet 216:1010-11, Oct 27, 1962.   C-215.
The Council and the press: Reegeles's comments,
  Tablet 215:640, July 1, 1961.   C-216.
The Council and the Word: constitution on divine
  revelation, America 114:283, Feb 26, 1966.   C-217.
The Council and unity, Eastern Churches Q
  14:251-2, Winter 1961.   C-218.
The Council at work: a digest of Catholic opinion,
  View 26:710, Dec 1962.   C-219.
Council begins: similarities and contrasts with
  1869-70, Tablet 216:982-3, Oct 20, 1962.   C-220.
"Council Bell" on display at the Vatican Pavilion,
  Magnificat 114:18, Nov 1964.   C-221.
Council call for change: on the adaptation and reno-
  vation of the religious life, America 113:559,
  Nov 13, 1965.   C-222.
The Council, Christ and you, Altar and Home
  2:46-50, Oct 1962.   C-223.
Council commission member: list of 160 elected
  members, Cath Mssngr 80:7, Oct 25, 1962.   C-224.

Council condemnation of communism? America
113:561, Nov 13, 1965. C-225.

Council, Curia and senate, Tablet 218:1159-60,
Oct 17, 1964; reply 1208, Oct 24. C-226.

Council decrees, Tablet 200:542, May 7, 1966. C-227.

Council discussions move from language to Eucharist,
Cath Mssngr 80:1, Nov 1, 1962. C-228.

Council draws nearer: pastorals of Abp Howard and
Cardinal Cushing, America 107:10-11, April 7,
1962. C-229.

Council experts muzzled, Tablet 218:334, Mar 21,
1964. C-230.

Council father's charges: changes in text of schema,
America 109:699-700, Nov 30, 1963; reply 110:42-3,
Jan 11, 1964. C-231.

Council fathers from Eastern Europe, Tablet 218:1125,
Oct 3, 1964. C-232.

Council: fourth session: symposium, Commonweal
82:685-96, Sept 24, 1965. C-233.

The Council in brief: sixteen major actions, Cath
Sch J 66:37-8, Feb 1966. C-234.

The Council in Chinese, Tablet 218:1067, Sept 19,
1964. C-235.

Council in crucial debate: don't oversimplify, Ave
98:12-13, Nov 23, 1963. C-236.

The Council in current writing, Doctrine and Life
11:606-13, Nov 1961. C-237.

Council is addressed to the world, Christ to the
World 7:429-39, 1962. C-238.

Council is divided on unity schema, Cath Mssngr
82:1, Nov 21, 1963. C-239.

The Council is now over, Clergy Rev 51:1-3, Jan
1966. C-240.

The Council: schema 2, Extensn 59:28, Jan 1965.   C-260.

Council should act on Jewish issue, Ave 99:16,
June 13, 1964.   C-261.

Council si, Commonweal 83:550, Feb 11, 1966.   C-262.

Council statistics, Tablet 218:1067, Sept 19, 1964.   C-263.

Council still in business, America 110:593, May 2,
1964.   C-264.

The Council: success or failure? Shield 43:39, Feb
1964.   C-265.

The Council: survey of readers' opinions, Jubilee
10:9-19, Oct 1962; replies 78, Dec.   C-266.

Council takes up Christian unity, Cath Mssngr 81:1,
Nov 29, 1962.   C-267.

Council to probe parish, America 107:233, May 12,
1962.   C-268.

Council week: press corps fight for bits of news,
Newsweek 60:99, Nov 5, 1962.   C-269.

The Council: who guides it? View 27:20-22, Oct 1963.   C-270.

Council's air of freedom stressed by Fr. Kung,
Cath Mssngr 81:1, March 21, 1963.   C-271.

Council's first topic: liturgy, Cath Mssngr 80:1,
Oct 25, 1962.   C-272.

Council's identity: implications of the sources of revelation debate, America 107:1165-6, Dec 1, 1962.   C-273.

The Council's momentum: accomplishments of the
preparatory period, America 107:522, July 21,
1962.   C-274.

The Council's press office, Tablet 216:956, Oct 13,
1962.   C-275.

Council's progress, America 109:550, Nov 9, 1963.   C-276.

Council's prospects, Time 80:80, Sept 14, 1962.   C-277.

The Council's statement on the Jews: a frank critique

by two Catholics and two Jews, Jubilee 13:36-41,
April 1966.   C-278.

Council's text on Jews in jeopardy, Christian Century
81:1548-9, Dec 16, 1964.   C-279.

Cousins, N., Pope John and his open window, Sat
Rev 46:20-2, Jan 19, 1963.   C-280.

Cousins, W., A head start toward unity, Hospital
Progress 47:108-11, Oct 1966.   C-281.

Covering the Council, America 107:290, May 26,
1962.   C-282.

Cowan, W., Vatican II: session I, Christianity and
Crisis 22:239-40, Jan 7, 1963.   C-283.

Cox, H., Underground churches: underground schools,
Commonweal 89:376-8, Dec 13, 1968.   C-284.

Coyle, A., Our Lady and Vatican II, Cord 14:131-8,
May 1964.   C-285.

Coyle, T., Doctrine on Mary and Vatican II, Marian
Library Studies 110:1-8, Nov 1964.   C-286.

Coyne, J., Media of social communication: text and
comment, Cath Educ 37:84, Feb 1967; 84, April.   C-287.

Crane, P., The range of social justice, Rev Social
Economy 16:89-108, Sept 1958.   C-288.

Cranny, T., Our Lady and the Council: further defini-
tion and the cause of unity, Ave 96:13-14, Sept 1,
1962.   C-289.

Cranny, T., Second Vatican Council and the unity
octave, Cath Sch J 63:45, Jan 1963.   C-290.

Cremin, P., The present Council, Irish Eccl Rev
99:73-82, Feb 1963.   C-291.

Cremin, P., Church Unity Week in Trinity College:
a symposium, Irish Eccl Rev 103:353-66, June
1965.   C-292.

50

Crichton, J., Church's Worship, 1964, Sheed and
  Ward, $5.00.   C-293.

Crichton, J., The constitution on the sacred liturgy,
  Am Bene Rev 15:46-63, March 1964.   C-294.

Crichton, J., The constitution on the sacred liturgy:
  pastoral possibilities, Liturgy 33:32-9, Apr 1964.   C-295.

Crichton, J., The general Council and liturgical reform, Clergy Rev 47:328-49, June 1962.   C-296.

Crichton, J., Liturgy in a dechristianized world,
  Liturgy 35:53-63, July 1966.   C-297.

Crichton, J., Vatican II: the second session, Liturgy
  33:7-11, Jan 1964.   C-298.

Crisis in authority: symposium, Critic 24:15-23,
  Feb 1966.   C-299.

Crisis in Rome: struggle between the bishops and
  the Roman Curia, Newsweek 62:76, Nov 25, 1963.   C-300.

Crittenden, B., Religious liberty: study in doctrinal
  development, Cath Wrld 200:354-5, March 1965.   C-301.

Crooker, R., Reply to Gregory Baum, Commonweal
  81:515-7, Jan 17, 1965.   C-302.

Crowe, M., The Church and religious freedom,
  Studies 55:255-68, Fall 1966.   C-303.

The crux of the Council: significance of the debate
  on ecumenism, Tablet 217:312-3, Dec 7, 1963.   C-304.

Cullman, O., Comments on the decree on ecumenism,
  Ecumenical Rev 17:93-112, April 1965.   C-305.

Cullman, O., Open doors of the Vatican Council,
  Union Sem Q Rev 20:107-13, Jan 1965.   C-306.

Cullman, O., Place of the Bible at the Council,
  J Biblical Literature 83:247-52, Sept 1964.   C-307.

Cullman, O., Press conference on the work of the
  Council, Unitas 14:287-96, Winter 1962.   C-308.

Cullman, O. , Vatican II: The New Direction, 1968,
Harper, $6.00.   C-309.

Cum magno dolore: latest curial maneuver, Time
84:88, Oct 23, 1964.   C-310.

Cummings, W. , The Council and the old-fashioned
Church, Liguorian 51:11-14, Sept 1963.   C-311.

Cunliffe, C. , The Council and liturgical language,
Life of the Spirit 16:280-87, Jan 1962.   C-312.

Cunneen, J. , Cross Currents: Looking toward the
Council, 1962, Herder and Herder, $1.95.   C-313.

Cunneen, J. , Looking toward the Council: a symposium,
Cross Currents 12:129-276, Spring 1962.   C-314.

Cunneen, J. , Realities of parish life: laymen and the
Council, Commonweal 76:298-300, June 15, 1962.   C-315.

Cunningham, M. , How can we renew ourselves?
Hospital Progress 48:65-69, March 1967.   C-316.

A cup of water: anti-poverty, war and Vatican
Council, America 111:643, Nov 21, 1964.   C-317.

Curious document: the Press Office's "A few themes
discussed in the Central Commission" Tablet
216:1038, Nov 3, 1962.   C-318.

Curley, F. , The second Vatican, Priest 18:593-6,
Huly 1962.   C-319.

Curran, C. , Some psychological aspects of Vatican II,
J Scientific Study of Religion 2:190-4, April 1963.   C-320.

Curran, C. , Vatican II: a new Christian self-concept,
J Religious Health 5:91-103, April 1966.   C-321.

Curran, E. , Vatican Council, Social Just 56:304,
Jan 1964.   C-322.

Curtayne, A. , The Council and women, Christus Rex
20:270-8, Oct 1966.   C-323.

Curtis, C., Decree on ecumenism: a Protestant
analysis, Cross and Crown 19:165-80, June 1967.   C-324.

Cushing, R., Prayer for success, Ave 90:11,
Aug 8, 1959.   C-325.

Cushing, R., Speaks to Vatican II, Cath Mssngr
82:5, Oct 8, 1964.   C-326.

Cushing, R., Two Council fathers, America 108:862-7,
June 15, 1963.   C-327.

Cushing, R., Why I spoke on liberty, Cath Mind
62:25-8, Dec 1964.   C-328.

Cushman, R., James A. Gray lectures on the Second
Vatican Council: Protestant report, Duke Div Rev
30:5-74, Winter 1965.   C-329.

Cushman, R., Protestant view of Vatican Council II
in retrospect, Duke Div R. 31:163-74, Autumn,
1966.   C-330.

Cushman, R., Reflections on Vatican II, second
session, Duke Div Rev 29:3-19, Winter 1964.   C-331.

Cushman, R., Roman Catholic renewal and Vatican
Council II: Protestant observer's view, Rev and
Exp 64:171-80, Spring 1967.   C-332.

Cushman, R., Some social implications of the Vatican
Council, High Sch J 49:132-8, Dec 1965.   C-333.

Cushman, R., Vatican II: a Protestant's view in retrospect, Lond Q 192:227-36, July 1967.   C-334.

Czech bishops at the Council, Tablet 219:1044,
Sept 18, 1965.   C-335.

Daly, B., Canadians talk to their cardinal, Ave
94:18, Nov 25, 1961.   D-1.

Daly, B., Communications decree, Cath Mssngr
82:8, March 12, 1964.   D-2.

Damiano, C. , Our schools, NCEA Bulletin 64:36-8,
    Aug 1967.   D-3.

D'Amour, O. , Vatican II on Christian education,
    Ave 104:20-2, Nov 12, 1966; reply 31, Dec 17.   D-4.

Daniel-Rops, H. , The Second Vatican Council, 1962,
    Hawthorn, $3. 50.   D-5.

Danielou, J. , On non-Christian religions, Critic
    25:46-7, Aug 1966.   D-6.

Danielou, J. , Le sujet de Schema 13: the Church in
    the modern world, Etudes 322:5-18, Jan 1965.   D-7.

The darkness of Christmas: Christ is the light of the
    nations, America 111:791, Dec 19, 1964.   D-8.

DaSilva, O. , The second session: was it really a
    failure? Way 20:40-3, Sept 1964.   D-9.

Daughters of St. Paul, The Catechism of Modern Man,
    1967, St. Paul Editions, $5. 95/$4. 95.   D-10.

Daughters of St. Paul, The Christ of Vatican II, 1968,
    St. Paul Editions, $2. 00/$1. 00.   D-11.

Daughters of St. Paul, Religious Life in the Light of
    Vatican II, 1967, St. Paul Editions, $4. 00/$3. 00.   D-12.

Daughters of St. Paul, The Sixteen Documents of
    Vatican II, 2nd ed with notes and index, 1967,
    St. Paul Editions, $1. 25.   D-13.

Davis, C. , The Church in the modern world, Tablet
    220:33-4, Jan 8, 1966.   D-14.

Davis, C. , The practice of referring everything to
    the Council is having a distorting influence, Clergy
    Rev 51:665-7, Sept 1966.   D-15.

Davis, C. , Recent books make the Council teaching
    accessible, Clergy Rev 51:329-31, May 1966.   D-16.

Davis, C. , The Vatican constitution on the Church,
    Clergy Rev 50:264-82, April 1965.   D-17.

Davis, H., A commentary on De Oecumenismo,
One in Christ 1:118-25, 1965.   D-18.

Davis, M., Ecumenism since Vatican II, Dublin Rev
516:160-4, Summer 1968.   D-19.

Davis, T., Americans at the Council, America
107:1172-4, Dec 1, 1962.   D-20.

Davis, T., Divine Word Press Service, America
110:176, Feb 8, 1964.   D-21.

Davis, T., Mr. Cartus in Harper's writes an anti-
Pauline article, America 113:248, Sept 11, 1965.   D-22.

Davis, T., The present revolution in the Church,
America 117:229, Sept 9, 1967.   D-23.

Davis, T., Reply to F. E. Cartus, America 113:248,
Sept 11, 1965.   D-24.

Davis, T., and Graham, R., Reports from Rome,
America 107:1126-8, Nov 24, 1962.   D-25.

De Iudaeis amended? Tablet 218:704, June 20, 1964.   D-26.

De Iudaeis: Israeli, Arab and Coptic reaction, Tablet
218:1388, Dec 5, 1964.   D-27.

De Iudaeis: the original and the revised versions,
Tablet 218:1093-4, Sept 26, 1964.   D-28.

De Iudaeis toned down? Tablet 218:1038, Sept 12 1964. D-29.

Deacons, collegiality okayed, Cath Mssngr 81:6,
Nov 7, 1963.   D-30.

Dearden, J., The Church and the modern world,
Economic Club of Detroit, 1966.   D-31.

Debate Ecclesia as session ends, Cath Mssngr 81:1,
Dec 6, 1962.   D-32.

Debate on deicide, Newsweek 64:86, Sept 28, 1964.   D-33.

Debate on revelation, Commonweal 77:269, Dec 7,
1962.   D-34.

Debate on religious freedom begins, Tablet 218:1095,
Sept 26, 1964.   D-35.

Debate on Schema 13, America 113:390, Oct 9,
1965.   D-36.

Decentralization: major Council issue, Cath Mssngr
81:9, Feb 21, 1963.   D-37.

Declaration on the Jews, America 113:5-6, July 3,
1965.   D-38.

Declaration on the Jews, Commonweal 83:112-3,
Oct 29, 1965.   D-39.

Declarations of Vatican II: see Constitutions C-178,
D-13.   D-40.

Decree of Vatican II on ecumenism: a symposium,
Furrow 16:3-20, Jan 1965.   D-41.

Decree on Christian Education, Cath Sch J 65:46-52,
Dec 1965; Cath Educ Rev 64:145-58, Mar 1966.   D-42.

The decree on the laity, Commonweal 83:262-3,
Dec 3, 1965.   D-43.

Decrees of Vatican II: see Constitutions C-178,
D-13.   D-44.

Deedy, J., Madison Ave religion, Critic 23:44-7,
Aug 1964.   D-45.

Deedy, J., Marriage and family in a new society,
Marriage 47:34-45, Aug 1965.   D-46.

Deedy, J., Missing dimension, America 104:590-2,
Feb 4, 1961.   D-47.

Deedy, J., News and views: key role of Cardinal
Lienart, Commonweal 88:90, April 12, 1968.   D-48.

DeFerrari, T., American Catholic Education and
Vatican II, Cath Educ Rev 63: 532-41, Nov 1965.   D-49.

DeGramont, S., Ecumenical Council: progress report,
Sat Eve Post 236:86-91, Feb 23, 1963.   D-50.

Dejaifve, G., Episcopal collegiality according to
Lumen Gentium, Lumen 20:637-50, Dec 1965.   D-51.

Delay on religious liberty: scandal, Ave 100:16,
Dec 5, 1964.   D-52.

Delegate observers at the first session: guests of
the secretariate, America 109:230, Sept 7, 1963.   D-53.

DeLetter, P., The second Vatican Council, Clergy
Monthly 24:49-57, March 1960.   D-54.

DeMarco, A., Key to the New Liturgical Constitution,
1964, Desclee, $2.50.   D-55.

DePagnier, R., Vatican secundum: two councils in
one, St. Augustine College Faculty Research J
2:74-84, May 1964.   D-56.

Deretz, J., and Nocent, A., Dictionary of the
Council, 1968, Corpus, $12.50.   D-57.

Derrick, C., Trimming the ark: towards a recovery
of perspective, Tablet 220:528-30, May 7, 1966.   D-58.

DeSoysa, C., Significance of the Vatican Council for
Christian unity, Church Q Rev 165:313-9, July
1964.   D-59.

DeSoysa, C., The Vatican Council, South East Asia
J Theol 6:64-72, July 1964.   D-60.

Details on the Ecumenical Council, Hom Past Rev
60:352-53, Jan 1960.   D-61.

Dialogue from top to bottom, America 115:678-9,
Nov 26, 1966.   D-62.

Dialogue in the Church clarified, America 113:662-3,
Nov 27, 1965.   D-63.

Dialogue with non-Christians: establishment of the
secretariate, Tablet 214:841, Sept 17, 1960.   D-64.

Diekmann, G., The constitution on the liturgy in
retrospect, Worship 40:408-23, Aug 1966.   D-65.

Diekmann, G., The full sign of the Eucharist, Nat
Liturg Wk, 25:86-94, 1964.   D-66.

Diekmann, G., James A Gray lectures on the
Second Vatican Council, Duke Divinity Rev
30:5-74, Winter 1965.   D-67.

Diener, P., A Protestant missionary's reaction
to the decree on missionary activity, Am Bene
Rev 19:57-63, March 1968.   D-68.

Digesting the Council: postconciliar climate in
Rome, Tablet 220:1296, Nov 19, 1966.   D-69.

Dillon, J., and Delaney, J., How do we cope with
the Council's effect on teen-agers? Ave 105:22-4,
April 15, 1967.   D-70.

Direction is a matter of discernment, option and
decision, New Blkfrs 49:115-6, Dec 1967.   D-71.

Disappointment: absence of Orthodox observers,
America 107:1080-81, Nov 17, 1962.   D-72.

Disease of irrelevance: parishes in eastern U.S.
seemingly not aware of the Council, Ave 98:17,
Oct 19, 1963.   D-73.

Document on Communism petitioned by 200 bishops,
Cath Mssngr 82:11, Dec 12, 1963.   D-74.

Documentine the general Council, Tablet 214:1005,
Oct 29, 1960.   D-75.

Documents and constitutions of Vatican II in pamphlet
form: N.C.W.C.; Daughters of St. Paul, and
Paulist Press; see Constitutions C-178.   D-76.

Dodds, R., Meeting away from home: how do we
implement the Council? Christian Century 83:92-4,
Jan 19, 1966.   D-77.

Doepfner, J., Cardinal Doepfner's views, America
108:714-5, May 18, 1963.   D-78.

Doepfner, J., Church and science in the world view
of the Council, Rev Politics 29:3-12, Jan 1967.   D-79.

Dogmatic Constitution: see Constituions C-178;
   D-13.   D-80.

Doi, M. , Implications of the Ecumenical Council
   for Catholic Protestant relations in mission work
   in Japan, Japan Christian Q 30:100-5, April 1964. D-81.

Doi, M. , Vatican II and ecumenism, Japan Christian
   Q 33:183-8, Summer 1967.   D-82.

Dollen, C. , Books on contemporary Catholicism,
   Luth Lib 11:2, 8 Spring 1969.   D-82a.

Dollen, C. , Charles Borromeo: hero of reform,
   Hom Past Rev 62:616-22, April 1962.   D-83.

Dollen, C. , Chicago, April 10: hope of the Church,
   Pastoral Life 15:147-52, March 1967.   D-84.

Dollen, C. , Civil Rights: a Source Book, 2nd ed,
   1966, St. Paul Editions, $.95.   D-85.

Dollen, C. , Gregory Barbarigo: symbol of reform
   today, Friar 22:31-4, Sept 1964.   D-86.

Dollen, C. , Liturgy the Art of Worship, San Diego
   Diocesan Liturg Comm, 1967, University of San
   Diego, $1. 50.   D-87.

Dollen, C. , Parish Bible vigils, Priest 24:758-61,
   Oct 1968.   D-88.

Dollen, C. , Pastoral liturgy's aggiornamento,
   Pastoral Life 12:5-10, March 1964.   D-89.

Dollen, C. , Will it work? Cath Lib Wrld 37:349-51,
   Feb 1966.   D-90.

Dolores, Sr. , Catholicism after the Council, Furrow
   18:119-21, Feb 1967.   D-91.

Dominian, J. , Vatican II and marriage, Clergy Rev
   52:19-35, Jan 1967; replies 223-5, March   D-92.

Donnelly, J. , Aggiornamento in Spain? Month
   36:21-8, July 1966.   D-93.

Donnelly, J., Collegiality: key to the Council
debates, Cath Mssngr 82:10, June 18, 1964.   D-94.

Donnelly, J., Summary of liberty schema, Cath
Mssngr 82:1, Oct 1, 1964.   D-95.

Donnelly, P., Council aims at Church renewal,
Direction 8:13-16, April 1962.   D-96.

Donovan, C., Vatican II's impact on education,
Publishers Weekly 190:21, Dec 12, 1966.   D-97.

Donovan, G., Vatican Council II: Its Challenge to
Education, 1967, Catholic University of America,
$2.95.   D-98.

Dorn, A., Teaching the ecumenical Council in the
secondary school, Cath Sch J 62:60-1, Sept 1962.   D-99.

Dougherty, J., The People of God, Bible Tdy
26:1804-7, Nov 1966.   D-100.

Dougherty, J., The postconciliar priest in the
light of St. Paul, Priest 24:106-14, Feb 1968.   D-101.

Douglass, J., The Council and the bomb, Commonweal 81:725-8, March 5, 1965.   D-102.

Down to brass tacks: the sources of revelation,
Tablet 216:1125-6, Nov 24, 1962.   D-103.

Dressman, R., Japan report: Buddhists at Vatican
Council II, Shield 45:16, Dec 1965.   D-104.

Drinan, R., Council will condemn anti-Semitism,
Interracial Rev 37:87, April 1964.   D-105.

Drinkwater, F., Conscience emergent, New Blkfrs
47:238-44, Feb 1966.   D-106.

Drinkwater, F., Reform and reunion, Today 17:23-25,
April 1962.   D-107.

Driscoll, J., Philosophy of Catholic education in a
time of change, Cath Sch J 67:29-33, Nov 1967.   D-108.

Duff, E., Anti-Semitism and liberty explained at the

Council, Cath Mssngr 82:1, Nov 28, 1963.   D-109.

Duff, E., Catholicism confronts the world, Social
Action 32:7-18, May 1966.   D-110.

Duff, E., The Council and a sense of renewal,
Guide 172:9-13, Nov 1962.   D-111.

Duff, E., Council sketchbook, U.S. Cath 31:6-13,
Oct 1965.   D-112.

Duff, E., Pope upset theories of Council pessimists,
Cath Mssngr 82:3, Dec 12, 1963.   D-113.

Duff, E., Vatican II, session 2, Christian Century
81:1057-61, Aug 19, 1964.   D-114.

Duff, E., and Nelson, C., Vatican II: second session,
1964, Nat Conference of Christians and Jews,
$.35.   D-115.

Duhart, C., Vatican II: Oriental prelate's view,
Liguorian 52:28-30, Oct 1964.   D-116.

Dulac, R., The Catholic's preparation for the
Council, Am Eccl Rev 141:145-54, Sept 1959.   D-117.

Dulles, A., The constitution on divine revelation
in ecumenical perspective, Am Eccl Rev 154:217-31,
April 1966.   D-118.

Dulles, A., The Council and the sources of revelation,
America 107:1176-7, Dec 1, 1962.   D-119.

Dulles, A., A Lutheran on the ecumenical Council,
America 107:626, Dec 1, 1962.   D-120.

Dulles, A., Protestant contribution to Catholic renewal, Hartford Q 7:7-17, Summer 1967.   D-121.

Dummett, M., How corrupt is the Church? New
Blkfrs 46:619-28, Aug 1965; replies 47:137-40,
Dec.   D-122.

Dumont, C., The decree on the Eastern Catholic
Churches, One in Christ I:334-8, 1965.   D-123.

61

Dumont, C., The forthcoming Council and
Christian unity, Unitas 11:37-45, Spring 1959.   D-124.

Dunigan, V., Who was Jules Isaac? Friar 25:2-7,
Feb 1966.   D-125.

Dunne, E., Is there anything in the liturgy constitution that concerns religious women? Sursum Corda
8:172-4, Aug 1964.   D-126.

Dushnyck, W., The ecumenical Council, Ukrainian
Q 19:300-14, Winter 1963.   D-127.

The duty of preaching Christ to non-Christians,
Christ to the World 12:470-8, # 6, 1967.   D-128.

Dwyer, G., The practical meaning of collegiality,
Tablet 219:1344-6, Dec 5, 1965.   D-129.

Dwyer, R., Recipe for being an extremist, Cath
Mssngr 82:10, Feb 13, 1964.   D-130.

Dyck, C., Literature of Vatican II, Anglican Theol
Rev 49:263-80, July 1967.   D-131.

Dynamic nature of the Church and of unity, Eastern
Churches Q 14:94-95, Summer 1961.   D-132.

The ebb of triumphalism? appearance and reality
in the Council chamber, Tablet 217:1197-8,
Nov 9, 1963.   E-1.

Eccevarria, R., Professional managers scan Vatican
II: AIM report, Hom Past Rev 63:693-6,
May 1963.   E-2.

Ecelby, N., On Scripture and tradition, One in
Christ 1:298-300, # 3 1965.   E-3.

Eckardt, A., End to the Christian-Jewish dialogue,
Christian Century 83:360-3, March 23, 1966;
393-5, March 30.   E-4.

Ecumenical Council, New Republic 104:4, Feb 9,
1959.   E-5.

Ecumenical Council, Newsweek 60:71-3, Oct 22,   E-6.
  1962.

The Ecumenical Council, Queens Work 55:12-13,
  Oct 1962.   E-7.

Ecumenical Council a challenge to Protestants:
  Luthern observer Skydsgaard, Unitas 14:224-5,
  Fall 1962.   E-8.

The Ecumenical Council and the evangelization of
  the world, Christ to the World 6:17-31, 150-65,
  304-14, 450-63, 1961; 7:14-29, 147-60, 1962.   E-9.

Ecumenical Council convened, Senior Scholastic
  81:18, Oct 24, 1962.   E-10.

Ecumenical Council: effect on book sales in three
  Catholic stores. Publishers Weekly 187:118-9,
  Feb 8, 1965.   E-11.

Ecumenical Council for unity, Social Just R 51:382,
  Mar 1959.   E-12.

The Ecumenical Council: Holland bishops, Social
  Just R 54:94, June 1961   E-13.

Ecumenical Council photos, Illus Lond News 241:593,
  596-7, Oct 20, 1962.   E-14.

The Ecumenical Council: significant texts and articles,
  Cath Mssngr suppl. Sept 13, 1962.   E-15.

Ecumenical Council: a special issue, Cath Dgst
  Nov 1962.   E-16.

Ecumenical next steps: world interchurch service
  proposed, Christian Century 80:483, April 17,
  1963.   E-17.

Ecumenical publication of Vatican Council documents,
  Publishers Weekly 189:68, Jan 10, 1966.   E-18.

Ecumenical publishing falters briefly in Los Angeles,
  Publishers Weekly 189:69, April 25, 1966.   E-19.

Ecumenicity of Vatican II, America 114:8, Jan 1,
   1966.   E-20.

Ecumenism: Schema 6, Extensn 59:27, Jan 1965.   E-21.

Efficiency urged in third session: Robert's Rules
   of Order, Christian Century 81:132-3, Jan 29,
   1964.   E-22.

Egan, J., Vatican Council II and the Reformation,
   Cath Mind 66:25-32, Jan 1968.   E-23.

Eichhorst, C., Report from Rome; fourth session,
   Dialog 5:58-64, Winter 1966.   E-24.

Eichhorst, C., Vatican II: how should we respond?
   Dialog 5:220-3, Summer 1966.   E-25.

The 84th supreme council meeting, Columbia 46:6-13,
   Oct 1966.   E-26.

Eldarov, G., Decree on missionary activities, Hom
   Past Rev 66:487-92, Mar 1966.   E-27.

Eldarov, G., Mission implications in the Vatican
   Council collegiality debate, Shield 44:26-8, Dec
   1964.   E-28.

Eldarov, G., Second Vatican Council and the missions,
   Shield 42:6-7, May 1963.   E-29.

Eldarov, G., Vatican Council II, Shield 43:14, Feb
   1964.   E-30.

Eldarov, G., Vatican Council II gave the Church a
   magna carta for the missions, Shield 45:1-2, Feb
   1966.   E-31.

Eldarov, G., Vatican Council II: its missionary
   record as the fourth session opens, Shield 45:4-5,
   Oct 1965.   E-32.

Eldarov, G., Vatican Council II: its service to
   missions, Shield 43:8-9, April 1964.   E-33.

Eldarov, G., Vatican Council II on non-Christian

religions, Shield 44:13-15, April 1965.   E-34.

Eleven point schema on peace and war, Cath Assn
Intr Peace 23:8-9, Dec 1962.   E-35.

Elko, N., Impact of the Ecumenical Council on the
vocational apostolate, NCEA Bulletin 59:494-6,
Aug 1962.   E-36.

Ellis, J., On the pathetic blackout: Paulist College
in Washington, D. C., America 112:305, Mar
1965.   E-37.

Elson, T., The Catholic Church battles its old
guard, Life 55:114-5, Oct 18, 1963.   E-38.

Elson, T., Pope John XXIII: 21st ecumenical Council,
Life 53:74-89, Oct 12, 1962.   E-39.

Emmet, P., The end of the post-conciliar era,
Critic 27:18-23, Oct 1968.   E-40.

End of session three: constitution de ecclesia,
Commonweal 81:339-40, Dec 4, 1964.   E-41.

End of term report, New Statesman 64:856, Dec 14,
1962.   E-42.

End of the Commission's fourth session, Tablet
216:243, March 10, 1962.   E-43.

End of the Counter-Reformation, Tablet 217:177-81,
Feb 16, 1963.   E-44.

The English bishops on Schema 13, Tablet 218:1244-5,
Oct 31, 1964.   E-45.

An enhanced authority, Tablet 219:1375-6, Dec 11,
1965.   E-46.

Episcopal Bp Higgins calls for prayers for the
success of the Vatican Council. Unitas 14:149-50,
Summer 1962.   E-47.

Episcopus, X. Rynne: gloom, doom and council,
America 110:224-5, Feb 15, 1964.   E-48.

Ernst, J., After the Council, Extensn 60:7-9,
Jan 1966.   E-49.

Ernst, J., Lumen Gentium: some aspects of the
Pilgrim Church, Tablet 221:205-6, Feb 25, 1967;
correction 245, March 4; reply 272-4, March 11. E-50.

Etteldorf, R., Council and Curia, America 109:234-5,
Sept 7, 1963; replies 336, Sept 28; 540, Nov 9.   E-51.

Evaluation of the second session, Cath Mssngr 82:1,
Dec 12, 1963.   E-52.

Evans, L., American lessons from the Council,
Tablet 221:1199-1200, Nov 18, 1967.   E-53.

Evans, L., Liturgical reform and the Council, Life
of the Spirit 18:404-12, April 1964.   E-54.

Everything's coming up roses, Ave. 100:16, Oct 17,
1964.   E-55.

Excess of zeal: Fenton's American Ecclesiastical
Review on Cardinal Ottaviani and the Council,
America 108:251, Feb 23, 1963.   E-56.

Experts for the Council, Tablet 216:943, Oct 6,
1962.   E-57.

Faddish, J., As eyes turn toward Rome, Cord
12:298-300, Oct 1962.   F-1.

Fagley, R., Vatican II and responsible parenthood,
Christian Century 82:332-3, March 17, 1965.   F-2.

Falardeau, E., The Indes and Vatican II, Cath Lib
Wrld 36:155-7, Nov 1964.   F-3.

Falconi, C., Pope John and the Ecumenical Council,
1964, World, $5.95.   F-4.

Familiarity with God, Social Just 56:375, Mar 1964. F-5.

Fannon, P., The Council and the Bible, Clergy Rev
48:539-49, Sept 1963.   F-6.

Farrell, A. , The Second Vatican Council, Clergy Rev
47:321-28, June 1962.   F-7.

Farrell, B. , Collegiality, Sign 44:56, Dec 1964.   F-8.

Farrell, B. , New teaching on Mary? Sign 44:57,
Dec 1964.   F-9.

Farrell, B. , Scripture and tradition, Sign 43:48,
Sept 1963.   F-10.

Farrell, F. , Vatican Council: end of the first phase,
Christianity Tdy 7:32-3, Jan 18, 1963.   F-11.

Farrell, M. , Objectives of the minor seminary in
the light of Vatican II, NCEA Bulletin 64:49-57,
Aug 1967.   F-12.

Father Kung now optimistic about the Council, Cath
Mssngr 81:7, Dec 13, 1962.   F-13.

Fathers in the modern world, Economist 213:687,
Nov 14, 1964.   F-14.

February: Catholic Press Month, Social Just 56:338-9,
Feb 1964.   F-15.

Felici, P. , Theological Commission on collegiality,
Cath Mssngr 83:5, Dec 24, 1964.   F-16.

Fennell, D. , The writer and the Church, Dublin Rev
516:99-105, Summer 1968.   F-17.

Fenton, J. , Cardinal Ottaviani and the Council, Am
Eccl Rev 148:44-53, Jan 1963.   F-18.

Fenton, J. , Revolutions in Catholic attitudes, Am
Eccl Rev 145:120-29, Aug 1961.   F-19.

Fenton, J. , The Roman Curia and the Ecumenical
Council, Am Eccl Rev 148:185-98, March 1963.   F-20.

Fenton, J. , Virtue of prudence and the success of
the Second Vatican Council, Am Eccl Rev 147:255-65,
Oct 1962.   F-21.

Ferrara, A. , The physician and Vatican II, Linacre
   35:216-8, Aug 1968.   F-22.

Fesquet, H. , Drama of Vatican II, 1967, Random
   $15.00.   F-23.

Fesquet, H. , Has Rome Converted?, 1968, Heineman,
   $4.95.   F-24.

Fey, H. , The pope and the press, Christian Century
   79:1347-8, Nov 7, 1962.   F-25.

Fey, H. , Splendor in St. Peter's, Christian Century
   79:1282-3, Oct 24, 1962.   F-26.

Fichtner, J. , The constitution on the Church: its
   forward thrust, Hom Past Rev 67:669-75, May
   1967.   F-27.

51 U.S. priests are Council experts, Cath Mssngr
   81:1, Feb 7, 1963.   F-28.

Final days of the Second Vatican Council, America
   113:255, Sept 11, 1965.   F-29.

Final vote on De Oecumenismo, Tablet 218:1182,
   Oct 17, 1964.   F-30.

Finn, T. , Peace, war and the Vatican Council, Cath
   Wrld 203:270-5, Aug 1966.   F-31.

First fruits in Rome: Pope to visit the Holy Land,
   America, 109:757, Dec 14, 1963.   F-32.

First fruits of the new Pentecost, Worship 38:378-80,
   May 1964.   F-33.

First session closes, Tablet 216:1217-18, Dec 15,
   1962.   F-34.

The first task: sense of what the Church is, Tablet
   218:1019-20, Sept 12, 1964.   F-35.

Fisher, D. , The Church in Transition, 1967, Fides,
   $3.95.   F-36.

Fisher, D. , The Council and reform, Christus Rex

20:7-19, Jan 1966.   F-37.

Fisher, D., The past is prologue, Cath Property
Administration 28:17, Feb 1964.   F-38.

Fisher, D., Christian unity sprinters, Sign 44:18-21,
Jan 1965.   F-39.

Fisher, D., Renewal in Europe, Cath Wrld 206:101-4,
Dec 1967.   F-40.

Fishman, L., Mater et Magistra, Western Economic
J 1:57-65, 1962.   F-41.

Flanagan, D., Mary, Mother of the Church, Doctrine
and Life 14:360-71, Aug 1964.   F-42.

Flanagan, D., The Second Vatican Council and Our
Lady, Irish Theol R 107:14-30, Jan 1967.   F-43.

Flanagan, N., The religious after Vatican II, Spiritual
Life 14:25-40, Spring 1968.   F-44.

Flannery, A., Chronicle: dates, facts and figures,
Doctrine and Life 11:499-502, Sept 1961.   F-45.

Flannery, A., Council diary, Doctrine and Life
13:533-8, Oct 1963.   F-46.

Flannery, A., Missions and Religious, 1968, Scepter,
21s.   F-47.

Flannery, A., Vatican II: The Church Constitution,
1966, Priory, $4.95.   F-48.

Flood, E., What price the Council? Clergy Rev
53:698-707, Sept 1968.   F-49.

Florit, E., Archbishop Florit and the laity, America
108:836-7, June 8, 1963.   F-50.

Florovsky, G., The forthcoming Council of the Roman
Church, Life of the Spirit 14:300-6, Jan 1960.   F-51.

Foote, P., Laymen: Vatican II's Decree on the
Apostolate of the Laity, 1967, Cath Action Federa-
tion of Chicago, $1.50.   F-52.

Foote, P. , Men and Nations: Vatican II's Pastoral
Constitution on the Church in the Modern World,
1967, Cath Action Federation of Chicago, $1.95.   F-53.

Foote, P. , World: Vatican II's Pastoral Constitution
on the Church in the Modern World, 1967, Cath
Action Federation of Chicago, $1.95.   F-54.

For the bowl games weekend: special to sport trends,
Rome, Dec 4, Christian Century 81:31, Jan 1,
1964.   F-55.

Forcella, E. , Religious liberty and the Vatican, New
Republic, 153:15-16, Oct 9, 1965.   F-56.

Ford, J. , Impact of Vatican II, 1967, Herder, $1.95 F-57.

Ford, J. , More on the Council and contraception,
America 114:553-7, April 16, 1966.   F-58.

Former president of Lutheran World Federation comments on the forthcoming Council, Unitas 11:147,
Summer 1959.   F-59.

Forster, A. , To pray in beauty, Musart 16:14,
April 1964.   F-60.

Forthcoming ecumenical Council an 'invitation to
unity' for Catholics, too, Cath Mssngr 77:8, March
12, 1959.   F-61.

Four Vatican decrees promulgated by the Pope, Cath
Sch J 66:16, Oct 1966.   F-62.

Fourth session, Time 86:74, Sept 10, 1965.   F-63.

Foy, F. , Long-range hope of the Council, Friar
17:39-42, March 1962.   F-64.

Foy, F. , What will the Council do? Friar 11:45-49,
June 1959.   F-65.

Francis Gabriel, Sr, The press and two Councils,
Columbia 45:8, Jan 1965.   F-66.

Franck, F. , Art and anti-art, America 108:419-20,

March 23, 1963.   F-67.

Franck, F., Faces at the Council, U.S. Cath 31:12-18,
    Sept 1965.   F-68.

Franck, F., On being human to the Council, Month
    36:10-21, July 1966.   F-69.

Franck, F., Outsider in the Vatican, 1965,
    Macmillan, $7.50.   F-70.

Frank, V., Through a glass darkly: a Soviet view
    of the Council, Tablet 216:1246, Dec 22, 1962.   F-71.

A franker atmosphere: goodbye to the cloak and
    dagger, Tablet 217:1086-7, Oct 12, 1963.   F-72.

Fransen, P., The Church in Council, Month Nov
    1963 - Feb 1964.   F-73.

Fransen, P., Episcopal conferences: crucial problem
    of the Council, Cross Currents 13:349-71, Summer
    1963.   F-74.

Fransen, P., Problem for the Council: episcopal
    conferences, Month 30:133-45, Sept 1963;
    197-209, Oct.   F-75.

Fransen, P., Theological implications of the discussion
    of the liturgy, Scot J. Theol 16:1-20, March 1963. F-76.

Fraser, H., Triumphalism of Vatican II, Triumph
    3:18-20, May 1968.   F-77.

Free expression in the Church, Tablet 221:255-6,
    March 11, 1967.   F-78.

Freedom and individualism, Month 34:335-6, Dec
    1965.   F-79.

French Protestant view of the Second Vatican
    Council, Tablet 216:92, Jan 27, 1962.   F-80.

Friedmann, R., Ecumenical dialogue between
    Anabaptists and Catholics, Mennonite Q Rev
    40:260-5, Oct 1966.   F-81.

Frings, J., Cardinal Frings on the Council, Tablet
    215:1192, Dec 9, 1961.   F-82.

Frings, J., The Council and the world today, Fran
    Herald 41:99-103, April 1962.   F-83.

Frisbie, R., Marriage and the Council, Marriage
    45:2-3, June 1963.   F-84.

From the whole inhabited world, America 100:540,
    Feb 7, 1959.   F-85.

Fruits of freedom: interpreting decrees and declara-
    tions, Commonweal 84:349-50, June 17, 1966.   F-86.

Fuentes, J., The liturgical reform of Vatican II,
    Philippine Studies 12:325-42, April 1964.   F-87.

A functional diaconate: document sent to all bishops
    by 82 signatories from 19 countries, Worship
    37:513-20, Aug 1963.   F-88.

Fusco, N., The Council and the Jews, Pastoral
    Life 12:27-32, May 1964.   F-89.

Fusco, N., French observers at the Council,
    Pastoral Life 11:30-2, May 1963.   F-90.

A future pope on the Council: Cardinal Montini's
    letters, Tablet 217:980-81, Sept 14, 1963.   F-91.

Gallagher, J., After the Council: back to school?
    Cath Wrld 200:28-33, Oct 1964.   G-1.

Gallagher, J., The constitution on the Church:
    liturgical comment, Worship 40:449-55, Aug 1966. G-2.

Gallen, J., Religious obedience in Vatican II, Rev
    for Religious 26:242-60, March 1967.   G-3.

Galli, M., and Moosbrugger, B., Council and the
    Future, 1966, McGraw, $10.95.   G-4.

Gamache, R., Spirit theology: problem in contemporary
    ecclesiology, Louvain Studies 1:323-42, Fall 1967. G-5.

Gard, P., The Greek Orthodox Church and the
Second Vatican Council, Unitas 14:269-81,
Winter 1962.   G-6.

Garver, S., Reflections on the Vatican Council,
Christianity Tdy 7:27-8, Dec 7, 1962.   G-7.

Geaney, D., Council reforms will change the role
of Catholic education, Cath Mssngr 83:13, Dec
17, 1964.   G-8.

The General Council, Christus Rex 16:123-5, June
1962.   G-9.

General secretary of WCC discussed Second Vatican
Council, Unitas 14:144-5, Summer 1962.   G-10.

Gensichen, H., Second Vatican Council's challenge
to Protestant missions, Intr Rev Missions 56:291-
309, July 1967.   G-11.

Geoghegan, R., Constitution on the liturgy: the Mass
in the immediate future, Furrow 15:93-6, Feb
1964.   G-12.

Georgiadis, H., Goodwill towards the East, Tablet
218:1429-30, Dec 19, 1964.   G-13.

Georgiadas, H., The Orthodox and our Council: the
reasons for their hesitance, Tablet 216:953-4,
Oct 13, 1962; replies 1054, Nov 3; 1168, Dec 1.   G-14.

Georgiadis, H., Orthodoxy and Roman Catholicism,
Lond Q 189:5-10, Jan 1964.   G-15.

Gerard, M., Documentation to direct religious education towards the service of the poor and all mankind, Lumen 18:65-78, March 1964.   G-16.

German bishops' pastoral, Herder 4:28-9, Jan 1967.   G-17.

German Protestant at the Council Secretariate,
Tablet 216:212, March 24, 1962.   G-18.

73

Gilbert, A., A Jew looks at the ecumenical Council,
Ave 94:5-7, Dec 9, 1961.   G-19.

Gilbert, A., Vatican Council and the Jews, 1968,
World, $6.95.   G-20.

Gilmour, P., Vatican II: great success or bitter
disappointment, Today 21:21-4, Oct 1965.   G-21.

Giordani, I., The place of the laity in the Church
in the light of Lumen Gentium, Unitas 17:195-216,
Fall 1965.   G-22.

The gnu and the ostrich: the need for breadth and
professionalism, Tablet 218:1281-2, Nov 14, 1964. G-23.

God's people face the future (series) Ave Sept 18 -
Nov 20, 1965.   G-24.

Good beginning, Commonweal 77:141, Nov 2, 1962.   G-25.

Good Council books, Sign 43:32-8, Oct 1963.   G-26.

Good, J., Observers at the Council, Furrow
14:310-14, May 1963.   G-27.

Good, J., The separated churches and ecclesial
communities, Irish Theol Q 32:150-6, April 1965. G-28.

Goodwill toward Rome, Newsweek 60:58, Aug 27,
1962.   G-29.

Gorman, R., Leave the window open, Sign 44:10,
Oct 1964.   G-30.

Gorman, R., More general Councils? Sign 45:6,
June 1966.   G-31.

Gorman, R., Reflections on the Council, Sign 45:8,
Feb 1966.   G-32.

Gorman, R., Reflections on the Council: unity in
diversity, Sign 42:6, Jan 1963.   G-33.

Gossman, F., Implementation of the conciliar decree
on ecumenism, Jurist 26:41-68, Jan 1966.   G-34.

The government of the missions, America 113,

660-61, Nov 27, 1965.   G-35.

Grabowski, S., The future of Vatican II, Way
   20:7-12, Nov 1964.   G-36.

Grabowski, S., The senate of priests, Pastoral Life
   25:19-24, Jan 1967.   G-37.

Graham, A., A dissenting view of Vatican II,
   Jubilee 13:36-40, Feb 1966; replies 14:4-5,
   May 1966.   G-38.

Graham, A., Pathos of Vatican II, Encounter
   25:16-22, Dec 1965.   G-39.

Graham, R., Church unity rounds a corner: non-
   Catholic delegate-observers to the Council,
   America 107:559, Aug 4, 1962.   G-40.

Graham, R., Civil rights in the Church, America
   109:257-60, Sept 14, 1963.   G-41.

Graham, R., The Council, the popes and peace,
   America 113:365-7, Oct 2, 1965.   G-42.

Graham, R., The laity and the Council, Cath Dgst
   27:16-20, Dec 1962.   G-43.

Graham, R., Laity, the Council and the new
   apostolate, America 105:246-49, May 6, 1961.   G-44.

Graham, R., Progress toward the Council, America
   104:110, Oct 22, 1960.   G-45.

Graham, R., and Nelson, C., Vatican Council, 1962,
   Nat Conference of Christians and Jews, $.45.   G-46.

A grand idea: lapel badge with symbol of Vatican II,
   Ave 98:17, Sept 14, 1963.   G-47.

Grant, F., The Council's unfinished business, Jubilee
   12:42-4, March 1965.   G-48.

Grant, F., Rome and Reunion, 1965, Oxford, $5.00 G-49.

Grass-roots collegiality, America 110:664, May 16,
   1964.   G-50.

Grasso, D., Motivation of missionary activity
according to the Council, Christ to the World
12:244-53, May 1967.   G-51.

Greater number of observers present for the fourth
session, Unitas 17:231-2, Fall 1965.   G-52.

Greek views of the Council, Tablet 219:369-70,
April 3, 1965.   G-53.

Greeks reject another Vatican invitation, Christian
Century 81:956, July 29, 1964.   G-54.

Greeks shun the Vatican Council, Christian Century
79:1186, Oct 3, 1962; 80:51-3, Jan 9, 1963.   G-55.

Greeley, A., The Church as new community, Sign
48:27-9, Nov 1968.   G-56.

Greeley, A., Four views of Rome: books which con-
tradict each other, Reporter 31:64, Sept 24, 1964.   G-57.

Greenacre, R., The constitution on the sacred liturgy:
reflections of an Anglican, Eastern Churches Q
16:338-44, Winter 1964.   G-58.

Gremillion, J., Pope Paul's other dialogue, Cath
Wrld 198:208-14, Jan 1964.   G-59.

Griffin, J., The Council and the marriage laws,
Priest 20:496-9, June 1964.   G-60.

Griffin, J., Time for a firm hand, Priest 24:780-84,
Oct 1968.   G-61.

Griffiths, B., Salvation outside the Church, Tablet
219:1409-10, Dec 18, 1965.   G-62.

Grimshaw, F., The new liturgical constitution: on
the use of the vernacular, Tablet 218:35-7, Jan 11,
1964; replies 79-80, Jan 18; 108, Jan 25.   G-63.

Groundwork for unity: the Council and dogma, America
107:876, Oct 13, 1962.   G-64.

Group 200, The Church Today, 1967, Paulist, $10.00.   G-65.

Guerry, E., Positive results of the first session
    of the Council for the evangelization of the world,
    Christ to the World 8:230-9, 1963.   G-66.

A guide to work on the schemas, The Pope Speaks
    9:306-15, 1964.   G-67.

Guinnessey, B., The popes and the Council, At-
    one-ment 7:7-18, 1965.   G-68.

Guitton, J., Auditor calls for ecumenical balance,
    Cath Mssngr 82:5, Dec 26, 1963.   G-69.

Guitton, J., Guitton at the Council, 1967, Franciscan
    Herald Press, $1.50.   G-70.

Guitton, J., Interview with Jean Guitton, Cath Wrld
    196:279-84, Frb 1963.   G-71.

Guitton, J., Two tendencies at the Council, Cath
    Mssngr 81:10, Dec 13, 1962.   G-72.

Guyot, G., The liturgical renewal and private devo-
    tions, Cath Mssngr 82:10, Nov 5, 1964.   G-73.

Guyot, G., Liturgy reform to mean change in semi-
    naries, Cath Mssngr 82:10, Sept 17, 1964; 10,
    Sept 24.   G-74.

Gy, P., Pastoral liturgy, Worship 37:550-63,
    Aug 1963.   G-75.

Hackett, J., The Council becoming aware of itself,
    Dominican 50:222-32, Fall 1965.   H-1.

Haes, P., Oecumenical Council, Lumen 17:609-22,
    Dec 1962.   H-2.

Hagan, W., The celebration of the Mass and the
    spiritual life, National Liturg Week 25:257-60,
    1964.   H-3.

Hakim, G., Hopes draft on Jews will go unchanged,
    Cath Mssngr 82:3, June 25, 1964.   H-4.

Hakim, G., No amendment to the statement on Jews,
Tablet 218:758, July 4, 1964.   H-5.

Hall, C., Roman Catholic Church's biggest challenge,
Readers Dgst 82:49-53, Jan 1963.   H-6.

Halligan, J., The Council speaks on the liturgy,
U. S. Cath 30:12-15, May 1964.   H-7.

Hallinan, P., American bishops at the Vatican
Councils, Cath Hist Rev 51:379-83, Oct 1965.   H-8.

Hallinan, P., An American view on liturgical
reform, Worship 37:547-50, Aug 1963.   H-9.

Hallinan, P., Common goal, America 116:11-14,
Jan 7, 1967.   H-10.

Hallinan, P., Reply to R. M. Brown, Commonweal
80:548, Aug 7, 1964.   H-11.

Hallinan, P., Toward our destiny, Sign 43:14-17,
Jan 1964.   H-12.

Hamell, P., The Second Vatican Council, Irish
Eccl Rev 98:156-60, Oct 1962.   H-13.

Hamer, J., New man at unity secretariate, Tablet
220:822, July 16, 1966.   H-14.

Hammer, R., Vatican Council and the Catholic Church
in Japan, Japanese Christian Q. 30:89-93,
April 1964.   H-15.

Hanahoe, E., Second Vatican Council and Christian
Unity, At-one-ment 5:117-18, 1963.   H-15a.

Hangartner, C., Implication for nursing education
from Vatican II, Hospital Progress 47:63-66;
108-111, Oct 1966.   H-16.

Hannan, P., Archbishop Hannan at the Council,
Priest 23:183-4, March 1966.   H-17.

Hanson, R., Third session of the Vatican Council,
Modern Churchman 9:192-6, April 1966.   H-18.

Hardon, J., The layman's place, Mission Dgst
21:27-31, Nov 1963.   H-19.

Hardon, J., The Second Vatican Council, Cath
Mind 58:196-208, June 1960.   H-20.

Hardy, E., Ecumenical Council in historical
perspective, Religion in Life 32:212-24, Spring
1963.   H-21.

Haring, B., The Church is laying aside the mantle
of royalty, Cath Mssngr 82:1, Dec 12, 1963.   H-22.

Haring, B., Family life draft ready for the Council:
birth control, Cath Mssngr 82:1, June 18, 1964.   H-23.

Haring, B., Johannine Council, 1966, Herder and
Herder, $3.50.   H-24.

Haring, B., Road to Renewal, 1966, Alba House,
$3.95, Image Books, $.95.   H-25.

Haring, B., The universal call to holiness, Hom
Past Rev 66:107-14, Nov 1965.   H-26.

Haring, B., Urgency of Council action on the Jews,
Cath Mssngr 82:12, May 7, 1964.   H-27.

Harkianakis, S., The ecclesiology of Vatican II:
an Orthodox summary, Diakonia 2:233-49, # 3,
1967.   H-28.

Hartdegen, S., The Council and secular institutes,
Sursum Corda 7:436-40, Aug 1963.   H-29.

Harty, M., Pastoral implications of the liturgy
constitution, Christus Rex 19:288-90, Oct 1965.   H-30.

Harvey, R., The Council, Friar 18:4-5, Oct 1962.   H-31.

Harvey, R., My brother's keeper, Friar 22:7-9,
Nov 1964.   H-32.

Harvey, R., That all may be one, Friar 14:12-17,
Aug 1960.   H-33.

Harvey, R., Vatican II, Friar 22:31-36, Oct 1964;
27-30, Nov 1964.   H-34.

Harvey, R., Vatican II: afterthoughts, Friar 22:6-8,
Dec 1964.   H-35.

Haselden, K., Charity the first step, Christian
Century 80:1539-40, Dec 11, 1963.   H-36.

Haselden, K., Third myth, Christian Century
80:1491-3, Dec 4, 1963.   H-37.

Hastings, A., A Concise Guide to the Documents
of the Second Vatican Council, 1968- Darton, vol 1,
17s 6d.   H-38.

Hastings, O., Catholic aggiornamento, Reporter
33:19-22, Dec 30, 1965.   H-39.

Hastings, O., Paul VI and the bishops, Reporter
29:23-5, Dec 19, 1963.   H-40.

Hastings, O., The Pope, the bishops and Edward
Gibbon, Reporter 31:22-5, Dec 31, 1964.   H-41.

Hathorn, R., Vatican II and marriage, Marriage
48:25-8, April 1966.   H-42.

Hay, C., Achievements in the first session, Sursum
Corda 7:292-7, Feb 1963.   H-43.

Hay, C., Apostles, bishops and the Council, Sursum
Corda 8:256-62, Dec 1964.   H-44.

Hay, C., The Council and Christian reunion, Sursum
Corda 7:98-104, June 1962.   H-45.

Hay, C., The Council and the laity, Sursum Corda
7:148-54, Aug 1962.   H-46.

Hay, C., The Council and the missions, Sursum
Corda 7:52-60, April 1962.   H-47.

Hay, C., The Council and the sources, Sursum Corda
7:388-94, June 1963.   H-48.

Hay, C., Council chronicle, Sursum Corda 7:340-7,
April 1963.   H-49.

Hay, C., Council: retrospect and prospect, Sursum
Corda 7:196-202, Oct 1962.   H-50.

Hay, C., The Council's divided vote, Sursum Corda
8:50-8, April 1964.   H-51.

Hay, C., Ecclesiological significance of the Decree
on Ecumenism, J Ecumenical Studies 3:343-53,
Spring 1966.   H-52.

Hay, C., The patrons of the Council, Sursum Corda
7:4-11, Feb 1962.   H-53.

Hay, C., Reflections on the liturgy constitution,
Sursum Corda 8:102-11, June 1964.   H-53.

Hayes, R., Bishop lauds Council results, Unitas
18:61-2, Spring 1966.   H-54.

Hayes, R., Collegiality, Cath Mssngr 83:1, Dec 10,
1964.   H-55.

Hayes, R., Interview on the Council, Cath Mssngr
81:1, Dec 20, 1962.   H-56.

Hebblethwaite, P., Atheists at the Council, Month
35:138-46, March 1966.   H-56a

Hebblethwaite, P., The coherence of the Council:
a guide to conciliar texts, Month 35:47-54, Jan
1966.   H-57.

Hebblethwaite, P., The Council Fathers and Atheism,
1967, Paulist, $.95.   H-58.

Hebblethwaite, P., Culture and kultur, Month 35:221-8,
April 1966.   H-59.

Hebbelthwaite, P., The people's pastor, Month
34:379-88, Dec 1965.   H-60.

Hebblethwaite, P., The possibility of peace, Month
35:103-11, Feb 1966.   H-61.

Hebblethwaite, P., The relevance of Schema 13,
Month 34:275-82, Nov 1965.   H-62.

Hebblethwaite, P., Religious life: sign and service,
Month 34:202-9, Oct 1965.   H-63.

Heenan, J., Calls for strong statement on Jews,
freedom, Cath Mssngr 82:5, Oct 8, 1964.   H-64.

Heenan, J., Catholics and the Council of Christians
and Jews, Wiseman R 238:3-7, Spring 1964.   H-65.

Heenan, J., Christians and Jews, Tablet 218:305-6,
March 14, 1964.   H-66.

Heenan, J., Council and Clergy, 1966, Chapman,
16s.   H-67.

Heenan, J., The Council and unity, Tablet 216:846,
Sept 8, 1962.   H-68.

Heenan, J., The Council and unity: those outside
the Church, Ave 97: 5-8, March 9, 1963.   H-69.

Heenan, J., The Council's greatest failure, Tablet
220:342, March 19, 1966.   H-70.

Heenan, J., De Iudaeis, Tablet 218:1125, Oct 3,
1964.   H-71.

Heenan, J., Splendid image of unity, Cath Mind
60:29-34, May 1962.   H-72.

Heenan, J., Two interventions on behalf of religious
liberty, Cath Wrld 202:176-7, Dec 1965.   H-73.

Heffernan, V., Outlines of the Documents of Vatican II,
1965, America, $.65.   H-74.

Heidbrink, J., Call to dynamic frontiers, Today
19:12-15, Oct 1963.   H-75.

Helbling, H., Second Vatican Council in history,
Orbis 10: 1257-69, Winter 1967.   H-76.

Helmsing, C., The rosary and the sacred liturgy,
Our Lady Dgst 19:199-202, Dec 1964.   H-77.

Helmsing, C. , Some reflections on growth in faith
in the post-conciliar period, Social Just 59:411-5,
Feb 1967.   H-78.

Hengsbach, F. , Two bishops speak, America 110:14-
15, Jan 4, 1964.   H-79.

Hengsbach, F. , The work ahead, America 110-15-16,
Jan 4, 1964.   H-80.

Hershcopf, J. , The Church and the Jews, American
Jewish Yearbook, 99-136, 1965.   H-81.

Heston, E. , Balance sheet on the Council, Ave
97:5-8, Feb 2, 1963.   H-82.

Heston, E. , The Press and Vatican II, 1967, Notre
Dame, $4.95.   H-83.

Heston, E. , Vatican II's Church of the future,
Columbia 46:12-15, Feb 1966.   H-84.

Hettinger, C. , Vatican II on the regulation of birth,
Hom Past Rev 69:198-202, Dec 1968.   H-85.

Hickey, J. , Vatican II and its proposals for seminaries, Nat Cath Educ Assn Bulletin 62:116-27,
Aug 1965.   H-86.

Higgins, G. , Sees drastic revision of Schema 13,
Cath Mssngr 83:2, Dec 3, 1964.   H-87.

Higgins, J. , Reflections on the first session of the
Council, Cath Educator 34:774-5, April 1964.   H-88.

Highest end: full freedom of conscience, Newsweek
64:102, Oct 5, 1964.   H-89.

Hildebrandt, F. , Methodist observer at the Second
Vatican Council, Doctrine and Life 13:199-201,
April 1963.   H-90.

Hill, E. , The word of God in the liturgy, Liturgy
33:81-6, Oct 1964.   H-91.

Hill, R. , Religious and the constitution De Ecclesia,
   Sponsa 36:227-34, April 1965.   H-92.
Hinson, G. , Reply to H. Buchanan, Christian Century
   81:1592-5, Dec 23, 1964.   H-93.
Hislop, I. , Aggiornamento: from dialogue to self-
   awareness, New Blkfrs 47: 101-3, Nov 1965.   H-94.
Historian poses freedom question: Msgr. Tracy Ellis,
   Cath Mssngr 81:10, June 6, 1963.   H-95.
Historic drama at the Vatican, N.Y. Times mag
   28-9, Oct 21, 1962.   H-96.
Hoffman, M. , Church and history in Vatican II's con-
   stitution on the Church: a Protestant perspective,
   Theol Studies 29:191-214, June 1968.   H-97.
Hoffman, P. , Rome and the confessional ecumenism,
   Luth Wrld 12:2:142-5, 1965.   H-98.
Hoffman, R. , The Council and the missions, Thomist
   27:537-50, Spr 1963.   H-99.
Hoffman, R. , The Church, the Council, the missions,
   Am Eccl Rev 150:102-17, Feb 1964.   H-100.
Hoffman, R. , Fears missions slighted by the Council,
   Cath Mssngr 82:101, Aug 4, 1964.   H-101.
Hogg, W. , Some background considerations for Ad
   Gentes, Intr Rev Missions 56:281-90, July 1967.   H-102.
Hohl, C. , Layman, Church and Council, Cath Book
   Reporter 2:7-9, Oct 1962.   H-103.
Holland, T. , Ecumenism at the Council, Eastern
   Churches Q 15:11-14, Fall 1963.   H-104.
Hollis, C. , Achievements of Vatican II, 1967,
   Hawthorn, $3.95.   H-105.
Hollis, C. , Vatican Council, Spectator 209:586,
   Oct 19, 1962.   H-106.

Holmes-Seidle, J. , What missionary bishops want
from the Council, St. Joseph magazine 64:21,
June 1963.   H-107.

Hope for Vatican II action on Jews, religious freedom,
Christian Century 81:628, May 13, 1964.   H-108.

Horton, D. , Looking ahead from Vatican II, Theol
and Life 9:260-71, Fall 1966.   H-109.

Horton, D. , Toward an Undivided Church, 1967,
Association, $2.50.   H-110.

Horton, D. , Vatican Diary, 4 vols. 1962-65, United
Church, $3.00 each.   H-111.

Hovda, R. , The paschal mystery and the liturgical
year, Nat Liturg Week 25:57-66, 1964.   H-112.

Hovda, R. , The recognition of the person, Nat
Liturg Week 25:221-5, 1964.   H-113.

How life will be different for Catholics, U.S. News
59:52-3, Dec 20, 1965.   H-114.

How rules changes affect U.S. Catholics, U.S. News
57:16, Dec 14, 1964.   H-115.

How the new Pope plans to modernize the Church,
U.S. News 55:46-8, Oct 14, 1963.   H-116.

How the Pope came to think of the Council, Tablet
216:483, May 19, 1962.   H-117.

How the press will cover the Council, Cath Mssngr
80:7, Oct 11, 1962.   H-118.

How to belittle the Pope, America 116:204, Feb 11,
1967.   H-119.

How to follow the second session: survey of periodical
coverage, Ave 98:18, Sept 14, 1963.   H-120.

How will they fit into the Curia: new post-conciliar
commissions, Tablet 221:80-1, Jan 21, 1967.   H-121.

Howard, E. , The Second Vatican Council and our
   separated brethen, Cath Mind 60:56-62, May 1962. H-122.

Howell, C. , The convent and the liturgy constitution,
   Sisters Tdy 37:146-67, Jan 1967.   H-123.

Hrolik, K. , Czechoslovak Church sees Council as a
   source of hope. Cath Mssngr 81:9, Aug 8, 1963. H-124.

Hughes,   E. , Revolution for Christmas, Newsweek
   66:11, Dec 27, 1965.   H-125.

Hughes, E. , Vatican II, scene two, Newsweek 62:27,
   Oct 7, 1963.   H-126.

Hughes, E. , Vatican II: striving for a new spring,
   Newsweek 64:55-7, Dec 14, 1964.   H-127.

Hughes, P. , The Council and the Bible, Christianity
   Tdy 12:9-12, Oct 27, 1967.   H-128.

Hughes, P. , The Council and Mary, Christianity Tdy
   12:7-10, Dec 8, 1967.   H-129.

Hughes, P. , The Council and religious freedom,
   Christianity Tdy 12:13-14, Jan 5, 1968.   H-130.

Hugo, J. , St. Augustine at Vatican II, Hom Past Rev
   67:765-72, June 1967.   H-131.

Humanizing theology: Fr. ·Bernard Haring on outmoded
   legalism, Ave 98:17, July 20, 1963.   H-132.

Hungarian bishops' pastoral, Tablet 216:1060,
   Nov 3, 1962.   H-133.

Hurley, D. , Africa and the Council, Commonweal
   79:10-12, Sept 27, 1963.   H-134.

Hurlet, D. , End of an era: rejection of the sources
   of revelation draft. Cath Mind 61:35-6, April
   1963.   H-135.

Hurley, D. , Freeing the word of God, Perspectives
   7:173-5, Dec 1962.   H-136.

Hurley, D. , Purposes of the Council: facing up to

the failings of the Church, Ave 98:30,
Nov 9, 1963.   H-137.

Hurley, D., Report from Rome, America 109:633-4,
Nov 16, 1963.   H-138.

Hurley, D., Second Vatican and racism, Interracial
Rev 36:236-7, Dec 1963.   H-139.

Hurley, D., and Cunnane, J., Vatican II on Priests
and Seminaries, 1967, Scepter, 21s.   H-140.

Hurley, M., The declaration on Christian education,
Hom Past Rev 66:224-7, Dec 1965.   H-141.

Hurley, M. Declaration on Christian Education,
1966, Paulist, $.75.   H-142.

Hurley, M., The ecumenism decree, Irish Eccl
Rev 105:12-26, Jan 1966.   H-143.

Hurley, M., The Vatican Council and the ecumenical
situation today, Irish Eccl Rev 98:28-42, July
1962.   H-144.

Hurley, M., Vatican II and Catholic education,
Senior Scholastic 88: supp 5, May 13, 1966.   H-145.

Hyslop, R., Religious liberty and social action,
Social Action 32:19-29, May 1966.   H-146.

Iakovos, Abp., Greek Orthodox Archbishop praises
Council, Tablet 217:1132, Oct 19, 1963.   I-1.

Icaza, J., They speak for married couples at the
Council, Sign 45:50-1, Dec 1965.   I-2.

Ilyin, B., The ecumenical Council: third session,
New Times (Russ.) 13-16, Dec 23, 1964.   I-3.

Ilyin, B., Troubles of the Catholic Church, New
Times (Russ.) 9-12, Dec 29, 1963.   I-4.

The impact of reform on the Church's laity, Ave
99:17, Feb 15, 1964.   I-5.

Imperious ecumenism, Christian Century 82: 1499-1500, Dec 8, 1965.   I-6.

India at the ecumenical Council, Clergy Monthly Supplement 6:345, Dec 1963.   I-7.

Innovation at Vatican II: fourth and probably final session, Newsweek 66:62, Sept 27, 1965.   I-8.

Inside and outside the Council: BBC's program: A breath of fresh air, Tablet 217:316, March 23, 1963.   I-9.

Inside the Council, Newsweek 63:54, June 22, 1964.   I-10.

Interfaith relations, Lamp 62:16-17, Jan 1964.   I-11.

Interim commission named by Pope John, Cath Mssngr 81:1, Dec 20, 1962.   I-12.

Interpreting the Council, Commonweal 77:584-5, March 1, 1963.   I-13.

Interracial Council: Bp Tracy asks race discrimination be declared unchristian, America 109:544, Nov 9, 1963.   I-14.

Into harbour: hopes and doubts at landfall, Tablet 219:1378-9, Dec 11, 1965.   I-15.

Iron curtain attitudes, Tablet 216:1000, Oct 20, 1962   I-16.

Is the Council premature? Cath Mssngr 80:3, Nov 15, 1962.   I-17.

Isacsson, A., The Council in Rome, Scapular 22:18-20, Feb 1963.   I-18.

Isacsson, A., Mary and the II Vatican Council, Scapular 23:3, July 1964.   I-19.

Israel and the Council, Tablet 218:686-7, June 20, 1964.   I-20.

Israel follows the Council, Tablet 216:1060, Nov 3, 1962.   I-21.

Israeli reaction, Tablet 218:1094, Sept 26, 1964.   I-22.

Iswolsky, H., Post-Conciliar trends and Eastern
    Orthodoxy, J Ecumenical Studies 4:125-8,
    Winter 1967.   I-23.

Italian Protestant, Vatican Council, Frontier 6:9-14,
    Spring 1963.   I-24.

The Italians at the Council, Tablet 218:1161-2,
    Oct 17, 1964.   I-25.

Iturrioz, D., The doctrinal authority of Vatican II,
    Theol Dgst 15:110-11, Summer 1967.   I-26.

Jackson, J., A Baptist view of Vatican II, Sign
    44:33-5, Sept 1964.   J-1.

Jaeger, L., Stand on Ecumenism, 1966, Kenedy,
    $4.95.   J-2.

Jancauskas, R., The concept of social justice, Rev
    of Social Economy 17:34-50, March 1959.   J-3.

Janssens, L., Freedom of Conscience and Religious
    Freedom, 1966, Alba, $3.95.   J-4.

Jarrett-Kerr, M., E pur si muove, Encounter
    27:56-8, Aug 1966.   J-5.

Jessup, J., Council ends its epochal task with a
    report, Life 59:22-9, Dec 17, 1965.   J-6.

Jesuit bishops at the Vatican Council, Interracial
    Rev 37:24, Jan 1964.   J-7.

Jesuit general's speech at the Vatican Council,
    America 113:429-30, Oct 16, 1965.   J-8.

Jesuit rejuvenation, Herder 4:118-21, April 1967.   J-9.

Jewish draft opposed by Arab Evangelical Church,
    Cath Mssngr 82:1, June 11, 1964.   J-10.

Jewish observer at the Council, Tablet 216:603-4,
    June 23, 1962.   J-11.

The Jewish statement, Commonweal 81:27-8,
    Oct 2, 1964.   J-12.

Jews absolved and other decisions, Newsweek 66:65,
    Oct 25, 1965.   J-13.

Jews absolved: responsibility for the death of Christ,
    Senior Scholastic 85:18, Dec 9, 1964.   J-14.

The Jews and Vatican II, America 109:698, Nov 30,
    1963.   J-15.

Jews express bitterness over charge of deicide:
    National Community Relations Council statement
    on the Vatican Council, Cath Mssngr 82:1,
    July 9, 1964.   J-16.

The Jews on the declaration, Month 35:90-2, Feb
    1966.   J-17.

Joblin, J., The Church in the world: a contribution
    to pluralism, Intr Labor Rev 93:459-76, May
    1966.   J-18.

Johannine Council, America 109:345 Sept 28, 1963.   J-19.

John XXIII Pope, Address after a Byzantine-Slav
    Rite Mass: preparation for the Council. The
    Pope Speaks 7:64-9, 1961.   J-20.

John XXIII Pope, Address at the closing of the
    Council's first session, Cath Mssngr 81:1,
    Dec 13, 1962.   J-21.

John XXIII Pope, Announcement: Quaesta Festiva,
    (Jan 25), The Pope Speaks 5:398-401, Fall 1959.   J-22.

John XXIII Pope, The closing of the Roman Synod:
    address, Australian Cath Rec 37:89-90, April
    1960.   J-23.

John XXIII Pope, Commissions established to pre-
    pare the Council, The Pope Speaks 6:240-3,
    Summer 1960.   J-24.

John XXIII Pope, Convocation of the Second Vatican
Council: Humanae Salutis, The Pope Speaks
7:353-61, 1961.   J-25.

John XXIII Pope, The Council and the renewal of
parish life, The Pope Speaks 8:188, 1962.   J-26.

John XXIII Pope, The dignity and the pastoral duty
of the bishop, The Pope Speaks 8:258, 1963.   J-27.

John XXIII Pope, Expectation of the Council:
promulgation of provisions to be observed:
Appropinquante Concilio, The Pope Speaks 8:105,
1962.   J-28.

John XXIII Pope, The great anticipation of the
Council, The Pope Speaks 8:105, 1962.   J-29.

John XXIII Pope, Letter to women religious, The
Pope Speaks 8:1-6, 1962.   J-30.

John XXIII Pope, Motu proprio: Oct 11, 1962 de-
signated as the opening date for the second Vatican
Council, Cath Mssngr 80:4, Feb 8, 1962.   J-31.

John XXIII Pope, Motu proprio on the conclusion of
the antepreparatory phase, Unitas 12:129-33,
Summer 1960.   J-32.

John XXIII Pope, On devotion to St Joseph, The
Pope Speaks 7:123-30, 1961.   J-33.

John XXIII Pope, Prayer for the success of the
Ecumenical Council, Marriage 43:33, Sept 1961.   J-34.

John XXIII Pope, Seminarians and the preparation
for the Council, The Pope Speaks 6:319-24, 1960. J-35.

John XXIII Pope, Special address for commission
members, The Pope Speaks 6:376-85, 1960.   J-36.

John XXIII Pope, To diplomats on the aim of the
Council, Cath Mssngr 80:10-18, Oct 18, 1962.   J-37.

John XXIII Pope, To employees of the Roman Con-
gregations, The Pope Speaks 8:105a, 1962.   J-38.

John XXIII Pope, To newsmen accredited to the
Council, Cath Mssngr 80:4, Nov 1, 1962.   J-39.

John XXIII Pope, To the Central Preparatory Commission, The Pope Speaks 8:70-4, 1962.   J-40.

John XXIII Pope, To the Central Preparatory Commission: progress, problems, Cath Mssngr 80:5,
Aug 16, 1962.   J-41.

John XXIII Pope, To the Council Fathers at the
solemn opening of the Council, Tablet 216:997-1000,
Oct 20, 1962.   J-42.

John XXIII Pope, To the International Congress of
Editors, Cath Mssngr 80:5, June 28, 1962.   J-43.

John XXIII Pope, To the Lenten preachers of Rome,
The Pope Speaks 8:38-48, 1962.   J-44.

John XXIII Pope, To the pilgrimage of the Salesian
Cooperators: the layman''s responsibility, Cath
Mssngr 80:5, June 28, 1962.   J-45.

John XXIII Pope, To the Secretariate for Promoting
Christian Unity on its foundation, The Pope Speaks
8:27-8, 1962.   J-46.

John XXIII Pope, Toward Christian unity, The Pope
Speaks, 6:231-9, Summer 1960.   J-47.

John XXIII Pope, Writings and speeches, The Pope
Speaks, vols 5 - 9.   J-48.

Johnson, H., The morally retarded, Social Just
55:231-2, Nov 1962.   J-49.

Johnson, H., Necessary distinction: renewal and
reunion, Social Just 55:194, Oct 1962.   J-50.

Johnson, H., Words and Vatican II, Social Just
57:154-5, Sept 1964.   J-51.

Johnson, K. , A Lutheran's view of Vatican II,
Priest 24:599-604, Aug 1968.   J-52.

Johnson, P. , Chaos in the Vatican, New Statesman
68:690, Nov 6, 1964.   J-53.

Johnson, P. , Reforming the scarlet woman, New
Statesman 64:480, Oct 12, 1962.   J-54.

Johnson, P. , Vatican and Kremlin, New Statesman
70:726, Nov 12, 1965.   J-55.

Jones, F. , The Second Vatican Council, Furrow
14:671-82, Nov 1963.   J-56.

Jordan, P. , Red suppression bars over hundred
bishops, Cath Mssngr 81:1, Nov 14, 1963.   J-57.

Jordan, P. , Viewpoint: the periti or consultants to
the Council Fathers, Magnificat 114:43-5, Dec
1964.   J-58.

Jordanian Catholics defend Council statement on the
Jews, Cath Mssngr 83:3, Dec 3, 1964.   J-59.

Jorday, P. , Recent Council actions show that most
Fathers want reform, Cath Mssngr 81:2, Nov 14,
1963.   J-60.

Jossua, J-P. , Yves Congar: Theology in the Service
of God's People, 1968, Priory, $5.95.   J-61.

Journet, H. , Little flock or immense people? Christ
to the World 12:104-11, March 1967.   J-62.

Joyce, T. , A good beginning, Today 20:29-31,
Nov 1964.   J-63.

Jubilee for Vatican Council's continued success,
Shield, 45:5, April 1966.   J-64.

Juda, Sr. M. , Ecumenical council day in the diocese
of Rockford, Ill. , Cath Sch J 62:52-3, Sept 1962. J-65.

Jung, E. , Table talk with the Russian observers,
Cath Wrld 196:273-8, Feb 1963.   J-66.

Jung, E., Women at the Council: spectators or
collaborators? Cath Wrld 200:277-84, Feb 1965.   J-67.

Kaiser, R., Pope, Council and World, 1963 Macmillan,
$4.95.   K-1.

Kaiser, R., The Vatican Council, Times Literary
Suppl v 2, 1964, Oxford.   K-2.

Kaiser, R., Vatican II, Act II: reportage, speculation
and gossip, Commonweal 80:517-8, July 24, 1964. K-3.

Kane, J., How tense are interreligious tensions?
Cath Wrld 197:351-8, Sept 1963.   K-4.

Kauffman, A., Reply to art. Pope's Ecumenical
Council, Christian Cent 76:363, March 25, 1959.   K-5.

Kaufman, L., Story of schema seventeen: the Church
in the present-day world, Cath Wrld 200:8-14,
Oct 1964.   K-6.

Kaufman, L., Vatican II and the training of
missionaries, Haythrop 8:398-404, Oct 1967.   K-7.

Kay, H., The Council and Christian unity, Christian
Order 3:590-94, Oct 1962.   K-8.

Kay, H., In a state of non-authority, Way Suppl,
5:78-88, Feb 1968.   K-9.

Kay, H., Vatican Council II: achievement and promise,
Month 32:105-11, Sept 1964.   K-10.

Keating, J., Mary in the Church, Guide 183:17,
Dec 1963.   K-11.

Keating, J., Theory of authority and Vatican II,
Worship 41:299-306, May 1967.   K-12.

Keegan, P., YCW Layman addresses the Council,
Apostolate 10:1-4, Summer 1964.   K-13.

Keeping the Council alive, Ave 96:24, Dec 29,
1962.   K-14.

Keldany, H., The A.B.C. of the Vatican Council,
  1962 Darton.   K-15.

Keldany, H., Understanding one another: some
  Anglican views on the Council, Clergy Rev
  48:12-20, Jan 1963.   K-16.

Kelley, D., Religious liberty toward consensus,
  Christian Cent 83:651-3, May 18, 1966.   K-17.

Kelley, G., Into the market place; Msgr. Kelly's
  resignation and the Council's press relations,
  America 107:841-42, Oct 6, 1962.   K-18.

Kelly, B., The decree on the church's missionary
  activity, Furrow 17:691-8, Nov 1966.   K-19.

Kelly, E.E., Newman, Vatican I and II and the
  Church today, Cath Wrld 202:291-7, Feb 1966.   K-20.

Kelly, W., Reflections on the status of a theology
  of the layman, Theol Stds 28:706-32, Dec 1967. K-21.

Kennedy, J.F., Letter to Pope John voicing hope
  for Council's success, Cath Mssngr 80:1,
  Oct 4, 1962.   K-22.

Kenneth, M. Sr., Renewal comes to New Market,
  Preaching 3:11-15, #2, 1968.   K-23.

Kenny, D., The Catholic Church and Freedom, 1968
  Tri-ocean, $6.00.   K-24.

Kerkhofs, J., Preponderances in the Ecumenical
  Council, Heythrop 1:232-34, July 1960.   K-25.

Kestel, E., The choir today, Cath Choirmaster
  50:102-3, Fall 1964.   K-26.

Kevane, E., ed. Allocution Publica haec sessio,
  Cath Educ Rev 64:159-67, March 1966.   K-27.

Key Council text on revelation, America 113:615,
  Nov 20, 1965.   K-28.

Keylock, L. R. , Ecumenical atmosphere: an
evangelical view of Vatican II, Christianity Tdy
7:30-2, April 12, 1963.   K-29.

King, J. , The decree on religious life, Hom Past
Rev 66-465-77, March 1966.   K-30.

King, J. , On ecumenism and on the Jews, Hom
Past Rev 65:481-8, March 1965.   K-31.

King, J. , Vatican II, Hom Past Rev 64:933-40,
Aug 1964.   K-32.

King, J. , Vatican II and religious liberty, Hom
Past Rev 65:388-95, Feb 1965.   K-33.

King, J. , Vatican II: collegiality; the schema "On
bishops and the rule of the diocese," Hom Past
Rev 64:674-81, May 1964.   K-34.

King, J. , Vatican II: De Ecclesia chapter II: collegiality and the diaconate, Hom Past Rev
64:571-80, April 1964.   K-35.

King, J. , Vatican II: lively encounters and vital
issues, Hom Past Rev 64:851-60, July 1964;
933-40, Aug 1964.   K-36.

King, J. , Vatican II: third session, Hom Past Rev
65:291-9, Jan 1965.   K-37.

King, J. , Vatican II to date, Hom Past Rev 63:567-74,
April 1963.   K-38.

Kissack, R. , Observing the second Vatican Council,
Lond Q & HR 188:204-9, July 1963.   K-39.

Kissack, R. , Vatican II: immediate pre-history and
the first session, Lond Q & HR 192:200-6,
July 1967.   K-40.

Klausier, A. P. , Ecumenical symposium, Christian
Cent 83-376-8, March 23, 1966.   K-41.

Klein, L., Unity decree basis for dialogue; Unitas
16:142, Summer 1964.   K-42.

Kleinz, J., Vatican II on religious freedom, Cath
Lawyer 13:180-97, Summer 1967.   K-43.

Klyber, A., Jews and the crucifixion of Christ,
Liquorian 54:33-6, April 1966.   K-44.

Kneeland, J.A., No laymen in the Council, Information 76:61-62, Nov 1962.   K-45.

Kneeland, J., Spirit of renewal calls for diocesan
and plenary councils, parish meetings, Cath Layman
78:2-3, Aug 1963.   K-46.

The Knowledge explosion, America 115:441, Oct 15,
1966.   K-47.

Kobler, J., Latin in the vortex of Vatican II,
Cath Educ 35:279-81, Nov 1964.   K-48.

Koenig, F., Austria's Cardinal at the Council,
America 108:671-2, May 11, 1963.   K-49.

Koenig, F., Card Koenig speaks on the Second Vatican
Council, Irish Ecc Rev 98:265-67, Nov 1962.   K-50.

Koenig, F., Our Lady and the Church; why the two
schemata were combined, Tablet 218:744, July 4,
1964.   K-51.

Koenig, F., Schema 17 held for 4th session? Cath
Mssngr 82:6, June 25, 1964.   K-52.

Koenig, F., Theological problems at the Second
Vatican Council, Cath Univ of Am Bull 32:3-4+,
July 1964.   K-53.

Koser, C., The II Vatican Council and Our Lady,
Marian Era 5:28-33+, 1964.   K-54.

Kossmann, W., Tuning in on the communications
decree, Cath Layman 78:12-15, April 1964.   K-55.

Krabbe, M.A. , The Ecumenical Council, Nuntius
   Aulae 42:11-25, 1960.   K-56.

Krasikov, A. , Soviet journalist's view of the
   Ecumenical Council, Curr Dgst Soviet Pr 14:15-16,
   Nov 28, 1962.   K-57.

Krol, J. , Third session of Council expected to condemn anti-Semitism, US Cath 30:52, May 1964.   K-58.

Kuehnelt-Leddihn, E. von, As the Council reconvenes,
   Nat Rev 14:452, June 4, 1963.   K-59.

Kumlien, G.D. , Council right and left, Commonweal
   79:362-3, Dec 20, 1963.   K-60.

Kumlien, G. , Eclipse of the Curia, Commonweal
   77:436-7, Jan 18, 1963.   K-61.

Kumlien, G.D. , Father Lombardi and the Curia,
   Commonweal 75:530-31, Feb 16, 1962.   K-62.

Kumlien, G.D. , A few surprises; clashes among the
   different groups, Commonweal 77:224-26, Nov 23,
   1962.   K-63.

Kung, H. , And after the Council, Commonweal
   82:619-23, Sept 3, 1965.   K-64.

Kung, H. , Can the Council fail? Commonweal
   75:621-2, Commonweal 75:621-2, March 9, 1962.   K-65.

Kung, H. , The Changing Church, 1965, Sheed, 9s.   K-66.

Kung, H. , The Council and reunion, Tablet 215:848-51
   Sept 9, 1961; 872-74 Sept 16, 1961.   K-67.

Kung, H. , Council: end or beginning? Commonweal
   81:631-7, Feb 12, 1965.   K-68.

Kung, H. , Council in Action, 1963 Sheed, $4.50.   K-69.

Kung, H. , Council, Reform and Reunion, 1962
   Sheed, $3.95 Image $.95.   K-70.

Kung, H. , Council Speeches of Vatican II, 1964
   Paulist, $1.25.   K-71.

98

Kung, H., Interview, Cath Wrld 197:159-63,
June 1963.   K-72.

Kung, H., Proposals: Opinion and the Council,
America 106:462-3, Jan 13, 1962.   K-73.

Kung, H., Objections to the Council, Jubilee
9:16-19, April 1962.   K-74.

Kung, H., Prospects for Christian unity improved
by Council's first session, Unitas 14:305-6,
Winter 1962.   K-75.

Kung, H., Reflections on the Council, Theol Dgst
11:65, Summer 1963.   K-76.

Kung, H., Truthfulness: the Future of the Church,
1968 Sheed and Ward, $4.50.   K-77.

Kung, H., What Christians expect of Vatican II,
Christianity & Crisis 23:156-60, Sept 16, 1963.   K-78.

Kung, H., What has the Council done? Commonweal
83:461-8, Jan 21, 1966.   K-79.

Labor weighs the Church: Canadian proposals for
the Council, America 106:847, March 31, 1962.   L-1.

Lackmann, F., What Rome started can't be stopped,
Cath Mssngr 81:7, March 7, 1963.   L-2.

LaDue, W., De episcoporum muneribus, Jurist
27:413-25, Oct 1967.   L-3.

Laity and the Council: concern of Permanent Committee of International Cath Organizations, Tablet
215:140, Feb 11, 1961.   L-4.

Laity in Rome, Newsweek 62:92, Nov 4, 1963.   L-5.

Lally urges media theology at session on Council
coverage, Cath J 15:1, July 1964.   L-6.

Lambert, R., A total view of parish life, Natl
Liturg Week 25:67-74, 1964.   L-7.

Lamont, D., The magna charta of the missions,
　　Tablet 219:1379-81, Dec 11, 1965.　　　　　　　L-8.
Language of the Council, Tablet 214:187, Feb 21,
　　1959.　　　　　　　　　　　　　　　　　　　　L-9.
Larkin, E., Religious life in the light of Vatican II,
　　Hom Past Rev 67:377-82, Feb 1967.　　　　　　L-10.
Last days of the Vatican Council's third session,
　　New Blkfrs 46:206-7, Jan 1965.　　　　　　　　L-11.
Last minute skullduggery, America 113:516,
　　Nov 6, 1965.　　　　　　　　　　　　　　　　　L-12.
Latourelle, R., Theology of Revelation, 1966
　　Alba, $9.50.　　　　　　　　　　　　　　　　　L-13.
Latourette, K.S., Vatican II: its background, its
　　character, its accomplishments to date, and its
　　prospects, Rev & Exp 287-300, Summer 1963.　　L-14.
Laubacher, J., Vatican II: looking back, Priest
　　22:535-41, July 1966.　　　　　　　　　　　　　L-15.
Lauck, A., What the Council had to say about art,
　　Liturg Art 32:111-14, Aug 1964; Reprint in Cath
　　Mind 62:39-46, Dec 1964.　　　　　　　　　　　L-16.
Laurentin, R., The Blessed Virgin at the Council,
　　Marian Library Studies 109:1-6, Oct 1964.　　　L-17.
Laurentin, R., Card. Cushing at the Council; Cath
　　Mind 62:26-7, Dec 1964.　　　　　　　　　　　　L-18.
Laurentin, R., Mary and Vatican II; Mary Tdy
　　55:43-8, Sept-Oct 1964.　　　　　　　　　　　　L-19.
Lawler, J.G., Shepherds of the Church; the Council
　　and a theology of the episcopal office and of the
　　lay state, Commonweal 76:394-96, July 13, 1962.　L-20.
Lawler, J.G., The Council must speak, Wrldview
　　7:40-5, Dec 1964.　　　　　　　　　　　　　　　L-21.
Lawrence, E., Liturgy's new life: first stage in

100

renewal, Ave 99:14-15, March 14, 1964.   L-22.

Lawrence, E., Revolution in the liturgy, Today
  19:8-11, May 1964.   L-23.

Lay representation at the Council? Tablet 216:436,
  May 5, 1962.   L-24.

Laymen and the Council, concerning chap. 4 of the
  Constitution on the Church, America 111:795-6,
  Dec 19, 1964.   L-25.

Laymen and the Second Vatican Council, Soc Just
  55:126, Aug 1962.   L-26.

Laymen at the Council? America 104:436, Jan 7,
  1961.   L-27.

Lazareth, W.H., The Church and change, Sat Rev
  47:38-9, July 18, 1964.   L-28.

Laxega, M., Report from Israel: a Jewish view of
  the Vatican Council, Jubilee 11:2-4, Feb 1964.   L-29.

Leahy, W., and Massimini, A.T., eds. Third Session
  Council Speeches, 1965 Paulist, $1.45.   L-30.

Lee, A.D., ed. Vatican II: The Theological Dimension,
  1963 Thomist, $5.00.   L-31.

Leeming, B., Hopes for Christian unity, Lamp
  61:5-7, Sept 1963.   L-32.

Leeming, B., Lutheran reflections on the Second
  Vatican Council, Heythrop 3:358-70, 1962.   L-33.

Leeming, B., The Vatican Council and Christian
  Unity, 1966 Harper, $7.95.   L-34.

Leetham, C., The decree on the apostolate of the
  laity, Hom Past Rev 66:385-95, Feb 1966.   L-35.

Leger, P.E., New Pentecost for the Church: renewal of Cath life, Cath Mssngr 79:5-6, Nov 16,
  1962.   L-36.

101

Leger, P. E. , Two Council Fathers, America
108:862-7, June 15, 1963.   L-37.

Leo, J. , Managing the news: American press panel,
Commonweal 81:5, Sept 25, 1964; Replies 102,
Oct 16, 1964.   L-38.

Leo, J. , Short-sighted treatment of the press,
Cath Mssngr 80:12, Nov 1, 1962.   L-39.

Leonard, G. B. , What chance Christian unity? Look
23:17-21, July 21, 1959.   L-40.

Leonard, H. V. , Vatican Council bibliography, Duke
Div Rev 30:77-9, Winter 1965.   L-41.

Leonard, W. J. , First fruits of the Spirit: Vatican
II's newly proclaimed Constitution on Sacred
Liturgy, America 109:798-801, Dec 21, 1963.   L-42.

Lercaro, G. , On communicatio in sacris with the
Orthodox, One in Christ, 1:187-9, 1965.   L-43.

Less ecumenism, please, Time 85:74, March 12,
1965.   L-44.

Letter from the Pope: Machiavellian intrigue of curia
conservatives, Newsweek 64:77, Oct 26, 1964.   L-45.

Letter, P. De. , The Council and ecumenism, Clergy
Monthly 25:410-15, Dec 1961.   L-46.

Letter, P. De. , The Council and the missions, Clergy
Monthly Suppl 6:221-7, June 1963.   L-47.

Letter, P. De. , Pontificate of Pope John XXIII,
Clergy Monthly 27:249-58, Aug 1963.   L-48.

Letter, P. De. , The preparation of the Council,
Clergy Monthly 25:13-22, Feb 1961.   L-49.

Levin, S. , The assistant pastor, Priest 22:346-7
May 1966.   L-50.

Liberality marks final discussions of second session,
Cath Mssngr 82:1, Dec 5, 1963.   L-51.

Liberty and the Council, America 108:186,
    Feb 9, 1963.   L-52.

Lichten, J., The Council declaration on the Jews,
    Cath Wrld 199:272-8, Aug 1964. Replies 200:71,
    Nov 1964.   L-53.

Lichten, J., A Jewish leader on the Vatican Council
    and the Jews. Cath Mssngr 82:5-6, April 2,
    1964.   L-54.

Lichten, J. L., Statement on the Jews, Cath Wrld
    202:357-63, March 1966.   L-55.

Lienart, A. Card., Visit with Cardinal Lienart,
    America 108:802-3, June 1, 1963.   L-56.

Limerick-Killaloe programme of sermon outlines on
    the constitution, Furrow 15:660-62, Oct 1964.   L-57.

Lindbeck, G. A., Church in the modern world; con-
    cerning books on the Council's teachings, Sat
    Rev 49:25-6, July 30, 1966.   L-58.

Lindbeck, G. A., Definitive look at Vatican II,
    Christianity & Cr 25:291-5, Jan 10, 1966.
    Reply: J. M. Oesterreicher, 26:133, June 13,
    1966.   L-59.

Lindbeck, G. A., ed. Dialogue on the Way, 1965
    Augsburg, $4.75.   L-60.

Lindbeck, G. A., Future of Roman Catholic theology,
    Dial 2:245-53, Summer 1963.   L-61.

Lindbeck, G. A., Impressions from Helsinki, Rome
    and Montreal, Cath Wrld 198:272-80, Feb 1964.   L-62.

Lindbeck, G. A., Jews, renewal and ecumenism, J
    Ecum Studies 2:471-3, Fall 1965.   L-63.

Lindbeck, G. A., Liturgical reform in the Second
    Vatican Council, Luth Wrld 10:161-71, April
    1963.   L-64.

Lindbeck, G. A., On Councils: impressions from
Helsinki, Rome and Montreal, Luth Wrld
11:37-48, Jan 1964.   L-65.

Lindbeck, G. A., Reform, but slow and cautious,
Concordia 35:284-6, May 1964.   L-66.

Lindbeck, G. A., Second Vatican Council, Christianity
& Cr 22:161-8, Oct 1, 1962.   L-67.

Link, M., A statement on teaching religion, America
116:16-20, Jan 7, 1967.   L-68.

List of official Council observers, Cath Mssngr
80:11, Oct 18, 1962.   L-69.

List of papal appointees to Council commissions,
Cath Mssngr 80:7, Nov 8, 1962.   L-70.

Littell, F. H., Pope's Ecumenical Council, Christian
Cent 76:224-5, Feb 25, 1959. Reply: A. W.
Kauffman, 76:363, March 25, 1959.   L-71.

Littell, F., The significance of the declaration on
religious liberty, J Ecum stds 5:326-37, Spring
1968.   L-72.

Little cause for alarm, answers to Card. Ottaviani,
Tablet 221:52-3, Jan 14, 1967.   L-73.

Liturgical agenda; persons appointed, Worship
34:631-32, Nov 1960.   L-74.

Liturgical challenge, America 110:135-6, Jan 25,
1964.   L-75.

Liturgical changes: concerning the Council's constitution on the sacred liturgy, America, 110:753,
May 30, 1964.   L-76.

Liturgical Conference, eds., Preaching the Liturgical
Renewal, 1964 The Conference, pb $1.95.   L-77.

Liturgical Conference, eds., Priest's Guide to
Parish Worship, 1964 Helicon, $4.50.   L-78.

Liturgical experimentation, America 116:304-5,
March 4, 1967.   L-79.

Liturgical renewal in the parish, symposium, Hom
Past Rev 64:1005-35, Sept 1964.   L-80.

The liturgy, Extensn 59:23-5, Jan 1965.   L-81.

Lohfink, N. , The truth of the Bible and historicity,
Theol Dgst 15:26-9, Spring 1967.   L-82.

Lomask, M. , Assignment to the Council, gr. 6-8,
1968, Doubleday $3.25.   L-83.

Lombardia, P. , Lay people in Church law, Irish
Eccl Rev 109:281-312, May 1968.   L-84.

Long, J. , East and West in the decree on ecumenism,
Unitas 17:3-16, Spring 1965.   L-85.

Lord Fisher's telegram for the Council, Tablet
216:995, Oct 20, 1962.   L-86.

Love, T. T. , De libertate religiosa: an interpretative
analysis, J Ch & State 8:30-48, Winter 1966.   L-87.

Lowery, D. , Birth control: what did the Council say?
Liguorian 54:19-23, April 1966.   L-88.

Lowery, D. , Vatican II: liturgical first fruits,
Liguorian 52:32-6, March 1964.   L-89.

Loyal opposition: reporting the Second Vatican Council,
Time 80:59, Nov 2, 1962.   L-90.

Lucas, B. , At the Vatican Council: the end of session
3, Spectator 213:700-1, Nov 27, 1964.   L-91.

Lucas, B. , Pope and bishops, Spectator 213:537,
Oct 23, 1964.   L-92.

Lucas, B. , Session 3: Vatican II, Spectator 213:328,
Sept 11, 1964.   L-93.

Lucky thirteen? schema on Church in the modern
world, Tablet 218:1193-4, Oct 24, 1964.   L-94.

Luke, Sr. M., The Council's message, Natl Cath
    Educ Assn Bulletin, 62:424-33, Aug 1965.   L-95.
Lunn, A., The coming Vatican Council, National Rev
    13:269-70, Oct 9, 1962.   L-96.
Lunn, A., Reflections on Vatican II: Christianity in
    a secularized world, Nat Rev 18:19-21, Jan 11,
    1966.   L-97.
Lutheran minister Lackmann praises the Council,
    Tablet 216:1144, Nov 24, 1962.   L-98.
Lutherans pray for Catholics; Bp Witte's prayer for
    the Council, Ave 96:17, Aug 18, 1962.   L-99.
Lutheran World Federation Committee discusses
    Vatican Council, Unitas 14:305, Winter 1962.   L-100.
Lynch, J.J., Council for the crisis, Friar 18:6-9,
    Dec 1962.   L-101.
Lynn, W.D., Second Vatican Council, So East Asia
    J Theol 4:27-32, Jan 1963.   L-102.
Lyons, B., Two years after Vatican II, Extensn
    62:7-9, Dec 1967.   L-103.

McAllister, L.G., Books on the Second Vatican
    Council, Encount 26:530-2, Autumn 1965.   M-1.
McAvoy, T.T., American Catholicism and the
    aggiornamento, Rev of Politics 30:275-91, July
    1968.   M-2.
McBrien, R.P., Do We Need the Church? 1969
    Harper & Row, $6.50.   M-3.
McCabe, B., American Jews and Vatican II, New
    Blkfrs 47:229-37, Feb 1966.   M-4.
McCarthy, C., After the noise, the hope of Vatican
    II, Christian Cent 83:167-70, Feb 9, 1966.   M-5.

McCormack, A., Proposed Vatican secretariate for world justice and development, Wrld Just 7:291-307, March 1966. M-6.

McCormick, J., Comments on the Council, Am Eccl Rev 149:431-3, Dec 1963. M-7.

McCormick, J., Membership, procedure, dress, etc. Am Eccl Rev 147:419-22, Dec 1962, 148:57-59, Jan 1963. M-8.

McCormick, R., The Council on contraception, America 114:47-8, Jan 8, 1966, Replies: 103 & 294, Jan 22, Feb 26, 1966. M-9.

McCorry, V.P., The Council as object-lesson in the theological virtues, America 107:912, Oct 13, 1962. M-10.

McCorry, V.P., God's purpose and the Council, America 107:826, Sept 29, 1962. M-11.

McCorry, V., A word from the citta eterna, Sacred Heart Mssngr 99:46-8, Jan 1964. M-12.

McCudden, J., In the interval: difference between the life of the Church in the Council and that same life outside the Council, Perspect 10:3, Jan-Feb 1965. M-13.

McDonagh, E., Freedom or Tolerance? 1967 Magi, $4.95. M-14.

McDonagh, E., The practice of ecumenism, Irish Theol Q 32:141-50, April 1965. M-15.

MacDonald, E., The challenge to change: decree on the apostolate of the laity, At-one 9:15-24, 1967. M-16.

McDonald, W.J., ed. General Council, 1962 Cath U, $3.50. M-17.

McDonnell, K., and Meinberg, C., Architecture and the Constitution on the liturgy, Liturg Art 34:2-6, Nov 1965. M-18.

McDonnell, K., The constitution on the liturgy as
an ecumenical document, Worship 41:486-97,
Oct 1967.   M-19.

McDonnell, K., Ecclesiology of John Calvin and
Vatican II, Relig in Life 36:542-56, Winter 1967.   M-20.

McEneaney, J., The other sacraments around the
Eucharist, National Liturg Week 25:40-47, 1964.   M-21.

McEntegart, B., Totality of outlook, Vital Speeches
29:299-300, March 1, 1963.   M-22.

MacEoin, G., The basic conflict within the Church,
Cath Mssngr 82:10 Nov 21, 1963.   M-23.

MacEoin, G., Powerful minority resists change,
Cath Mssngr 81:10, Nov 14, 1963.   M-24.

MacEoin, G., Vatican II is for you, Queenswork
56:6-8, Jan 1964.   M-25.

MacEoin, G., What Happened at Rome? 1966 Holt,
$4.95, Doubleday, $.85.   M-26.

MacEoin, G., Your world and mine; a series on
the Council, see issues of Cath Mssngr Oct 3,
1963-Nov 21, 1963.   M-27.

McGarry, C., Collegiality and catholicity, Irish
Theol Q 32:189-208, July 1965.   M-28.

McGarry, C., Salt of the earth and light of the
world, Studies 54:113-30, Sum-Fall 1965.   M-29.

McGoldrick, P., The constitution on the Church,
Furrow 17:148-55, March 1966.   M-30.

McGrath, G., The Church and social revolution in
Latin America, Perspective 10:4-10, Jan-Feb
1965.   M-31.

McGrath, J., Canon Law for the Church and the
Churches, Jurist 26:454-9, Oct 1966.   M-32.

McGrath, M., Impressions of the Council, America

113:182-3, Aug 21, 1965.   M-33.

McGurn, B., Essentials of reunion, Cath Dgst
27:117-22, Jan 1963.   M-34.

McHugh, J., Vatican II and marriage, Ave
106:20-23, Aug 26, 1967.   M-35.

Mack, P., Advice to journalists; address of Pope
John and Bp Sheen, View 26:11-13, Dec 1962.   M-36.

McKee, A.F., The market principle and Roman
Catholic thought, Kyklos, 17:65-80, 1964.   M-37.

McKeon, R., Mary, the Council and reunion, Mary
Tdy 57:2-8, Sept-Oct 1966.   M-38.

McKeon, R., The second Vatican Council and the
common good, Am Eccl Rev 157:736-42, July
1967.   M-39.

McKeon, R., Vatican Council and values, Soc Just
61:161-4, Sept 1968.   M-40.

Mackin, T., Vatican II, contraception and Christian
marriage, America 117:54-7; 117:314-17, July 15,
1967; Sept 23, 1967.   M-41.

McManus, F.,   Changes in the liturgy: constitution
on worship, Commonweal 79:594-6, Feb 14, 1964. M-42.

McManus, F.,   Coming reforms in the liturgy,
Cath Wrld 196:335-42, March 1963.   M-43.

McManus, F., A commentary on the Dogmatic Constitution on the Sacred Liturgy, Liturg Arts
36:34-6, Feb 1968.   M-44.

McManus, F., The Constitution on the Liturgy:
commentary, Worship 38:314-17, May 1964;
450-96, Aug-Sept 1964; 515-65, Oct 1964.   M-45.

McManus, F., The Council, the press and the
liturgy, Cath Journalist 15:13-14+, July 1964.   M-46.

McManus, F., Ecumenical import of the Constitution on the liturgy, Studia Lit 4:1-8,
Spring 1965. M-47.

McManus, F., How long for Council reforms to
go into effect? Worship 37:623-4, Oct 1963. M-48.

McManus, F., Liturgical reform provided for by
the Ecumenical Council, issues of Cath Mssngr
Dec 26, 1963-Feb 27, 1964. M-49.

McManus, F., Recent documents on church architecture, Liturg Arts 33:80, May 1965. M-50.

McManus, F., Sacramental Liturgy, 1967
Herder and Herder, $4.95. M-51.

McManus, F., Second Vatican Council and the
canon law, Jurist 22:259-86, July 1962. M-52.

McManus, F., Vatican Council II, Worship
37:140-53, Feb 1963. M-53.

McManus, M., The American Law on Religious
Freedom as Viewed in the Declaration on Religious
Freedom of the Second Vatican Council, 1967
(Rome) Cath Book Agency, Thesis. M-54.

McNally, R., The word of God and the mystery of
Christ, Worship 38:392-402, June-July 1964. M-55.

McNamara, K., Catholic principles, Irish Theol Q
32:129-40, April 1965. M-56.

McNamara, K., The catholicity of Vatican II, Irish
Eccl Rev 103:367-80, June 1965. M-57.

McNamara, K., The Church and the Council;
perfecting the four properties of the Church,
Furrow 14:282-302, May 1963. M-58.

McNamara, K., Ecumenism in the light of Vatican II,
Irish Eccl Rev 105:137-52, March 1966. M-59.

McNamara, K., The mystery of the Church, Irish
  Eccl Rev 106:82-103, Aug 1966.   M-60.
McNamara, K., ed. Vatican II, The Constitution of
  the Church, 1968 Chapman, 63s.   M-61.
MacNamara, V., Vatican II and missionary
  spirituality, Furrow 19:247-55, May 1968.   M-62.
McNaspy, C. J., Art and anti-art: concerning drawings
  of Vatican Council II by F. Franck, America
  109:419-20 March 23, 1963.   M-63.
McNaspy, C., Chapter on liturgical art, Liturg
  Art 32:37, Feb 1964.   M-64.
McNaspy, C., The Council and the liturgy,
  America 111:778, Dec 12, 1964.   M-65.
McNaspy, C., Important religious events of 1965,
  America 114:58, Jan 15, 1966.   M-66.
McNaspy, C. J., Liturgy: barrier or bond? Council's
  Constitution on the Liturgy, America 110:278-80,
  Feb 29, 1964.   M-67.
McNaspy, C. J., Music at the Council, America
  107:1278-79, Dec 29, 1962.   M-68.
McNaspy, C., Music of the people in sacred
  worship, Natl Liturg Week 25:198-204, 1964.   M-69.
McNaspy, C. J., Our Changing Liturgy, 1966
  Hawthorn, $4.95.   M-70.
McNaspy, C. J., Three giant steps, America
  111:776-8, Dec 12, 1964.   M-71.
McNaspy, C. J., Vatican II and art, America
  110:126-7, Jan 18, 1964.   M-72.
McNaspy, C. J., Vatican II on music: Constitution
  on the Sacred Liturgy, America 110:55-6,
  Jan 11, 1964.   M-73.

McNicholl, A., Approaches to Vatican II,
Christian Order 4:624-40, Oct 1963.   M-74.

McNicholl, A., At the Council, Doctrine & Life
13:623-40, Dec 1963.   M-75.

McNicholl, A., The Church in the world today,
Irish Eccl Rev 103:138-47, March 1965.   M-76.

McNicholl, A., Dynamics of the Council, Irish
Eccl Rev 105:209-31, April 1966.   M-77.

McNicholl, A., Looking back on the Council, Irish
Eccl Rev 105:153-72, March 1966.   M-78.

McNicholl, A., Vatican II: third session, Thomist
29:79-113, Jan 1965.   M-79.

McQuilkin, F., Reforming the reformed liturgy,
Past Life 25:9-12, Jan 1967.   M-80.

McRedmond, J., The journalist, Furrow 15:1-13,
Jan 1964.   M-81.

McSorley, H. J., Luther, Trent, Vatican I and II,
McCormick Q 21:95-104, Nov 1967.   M-82.

Madden, D., Home-in-Rome: American bishops'
office at the Council, Columbia 43:17-19+
Feb 1963.   M-83.

Madden, D., Women at the Council, Cath Dgst
29:16-9, April 1965.   M-84.

Made in the U.S.A. bishops and the Council debate
on religious liberty, Extensn 59:10, Dec 1964.   M-85.

Madsen, C., On the constitution on the sacred
liturgy, see issues of Cath Mssngr Feb 13,
1964, April 9, 1964.   M-86.

Maguire, J.B., Uniting East and West, Ave
89:18, Feb 14, 1959.   M-87.

Malatesta, E., Pope John Council and the prayer
of Christ, Month 28:261-63, Nov 1962.   M-88.

Maloney, J., Coming of age; the maturing of the
Church, Today 20:2, Dec 1964.   M-89.

Maly, E.H., The Council and divine revelation,
Hartford Q 6:6-19, Summer 1966.   M-90.

Maly, E., The liturgical constitution, Bible Tdy
10:616-22, Feb 1964.   M-91.

Maly, E., Report on the general themes discussed
by the Council Fathers, Bible Tdy 9:546-51,
Dec 1963.   M-92.

Maly, K., A seminarian looks at the Council,
Hom Past Rev 65:127-33, Nov 1964.   M-93.

Mannion, J.B., First, the liturgy; hopes for reforms
by the Council, Commonweal 76:346-48, June 29,
1962.   M-94.

Mannion, J., High Church-low Church liturgical
renewal in the United States, Am Eccl Rev
151:386-92, Dec 1964.   M-95.

Mannion, J., A liturgical bedtime story, Cath
Layman 78:17-24, Aug 1964.   M-96.

Mannion, J.B., Need for reform: constitution on
the liturgy, Commonweal 78:495-7, Aug 23, 1963. M-97.

Manz, J.G., Vatican II: renewal or reform? 1966
Concordia, $1.95.   M-98.

Marcellus, Reply to J.B. Sheerin, Cath Wrld
202:194, Jan 1966.   M-99.

Marck, W., Toward a renewal of the theology of
marriage, Thomist 30:307-42, Oct 1966.   M-100.

Marie Aimee, M., Vatican II and the Pentecostal
spirit, Marriage 48:38-43, June 1966.   M-101.

Maritain, J., Some reflections on the Council,
Reporter 38:32-6, Feb 8, 1968.   M-102.

113

Marjorie, Sr. , Anguish in the aggiornamento,
Spir Life 12:256-9, Winter 1966.   M-103.

Markus, R. , The tradition of christendom and the
second Vatican Council, New Blkfrs 46:322-9,
March 1965.   M-104.

Marle, R. , The Council: the limits of aggiornamento,
Studies 52:27-36, Spring 1963.   M-105.

Marshall, J. , The Council and the Commission,
Tablet 222:933-4, Sept 21, 1968.   M-106.

Martin, A. , Thoughts on the General Council,
Friar 21:31, Jan 1964; 34-42-Feb 1964.   M-107.

Marty, M. E. , Collegiality: the lid is off, Christian
Cent 81:1552-3, Dec 16, 1964.   M-108.

Marty, M. E. , Council politics at dead end, Christian
Cent 81:1519-20, Dec 9, 1964.   M-109.

Marty, M.E.,On primacy: thinking the unthinkable,
Cath Wrld 202:26-31, Oct 1965.   M-110.

Marty, M. E. , Vatican II was just the beginning,
Christian Cent 83:455-7, April 13, 1966.   M-111.

Marty, M.E. , We have a Council, Christian Cent
81:1483, 89-90, Dec 2, 1964.   M-112.

Marx, M. , The altar of the sacrifice banquet, Natl
Liturg Week 25:155-60, 1964.   M-113.

Mary and the Church, America 111:5, July 4, 1964.   M-114.

Mary and the Church, Marian Era 5:114-20, 1964.   M-115.

Mary Teresa, Sr. , American Catholic education
and Vatican Council II, Cath Educ Rev 63:532-41,
Nov 1965.   M-116.

Mary Teresa, Sr., Pastoral constitution on the
Church in the modern world, Cath Sch J 68:63-5,
Feb 1968.   M-117.

Mary Teresa, Sr., Study the declaration on
christian education, Cath Sch J 67:44-5,
June 1967.   M-118.

Mary Teresa, Sr., A teacher's guide to the constitution on divine revelation, Cath Sch J
67:83-4, March 1967.   M-119.

Mascall, E., Vatican II on the Church and ecumenism:
Anglican comment, New Blkfrs 46:386-95,
April 1965.   M-120.

Mass media and Council, America 107:105-06,
April 28, 1962.   M-121.

The mass media decree under fire; Catholic Press
convention in Pittsburgh, Tablet 218:676, June 13,
1964.   M-122.

Masse, B. L., Vatican on social progress, America
114:776-8, May 28, 1966.   M-123.

Masterson, R., Comparison of the Vatican Council's
import with that of the present revolution of the
American Negro, Cross and Crown 16:259-61,
Sept 1964.   M-124.

Masterson, R., The Council and the message of
Bethlehem, Cross and Crown 14:387-89, Dec 1962. M-125.

Matzerath, R., Decree on ecumenism officially
ends counter-reformation, Cath Mssngr 83:14,
Dec 17, 1964; 8, Dec 24, 1964.   M-126.

Matzerath, R., Pope John, St. Francis and
Vatican II, Way 19:5-12, Oct 1963.   M-127.

Maximos IV, Patriarch, an appeal for clarity,
Jubilee 12:41-2, March 1965.   M-128.

Maximos IV., Patriarch, collegiality, the Curia and
the east, Tablet 218:592, May 23, 1964.   M-129.

Maximos IV, Patriarch Maximos IV and Vatican
Council II, Cath Wrld 198:372-9, March 1964.   M-130.

Maynard, F., The third session, Way 20:27-30,
Nov 1964.   M-131.

Mayor, F., Vatican II before schema 17, Realites
46-53, April 1964.   M-132.

Meade, D., Protestants and the Council, US Cath
30:14-24, Oct 1964.   M-133.

Meeting the world, schema 13 takes final shape,
Tablet 219:1319-21, Nov 27, 1965.   M-134.

Meinhold, P., The Council so far; a protestant
evaluation, Cross Currents 13:324-34, Summer
1963.   M-135.

Meinhold, P., The protestant and the Council,
Cross Currents 10:125-37, Spring 1960.   M-136.

Menges, R., Roundup on ecumenism, Extensn
61:5-7, Nov 1966.   M-137.

Merton, T., The Council and religious life, New
Blkfrs 47:5-17, Oct 1965.   M-138.

Message to mankind, America 107:971, Nov 3,
1962.   M-139.

Message to the world: call for peace, social justice
and the realization of the brotherhood of man,
Tablet 216:1028, Oct 27, 1962.   M-140.

Meyendorff, J., Papacy: an issue the Vatican Council
skirted, Orthodox view, Christianity Tdy 10:6-9,
March 18, 1966.   M-141.

Meyendorff, J., Towards the Roman Council, St
Vlad Sem Q 5 - 3:45-7, 1961.   M-142.

Meyendorff, J., Vatican II: a preliminary reaction,
St Vlad Sem Q 9 - 1:26-7, 1961.   M-143.

Meyendorff, J., Vatican II: definitions or search

116

for unity, St Vlad Sem Q 7 - 4:164-8, 1963. M-144.

Meyer, Card. A.G., Lenten pastoral, 1962 Cath
Mssngr 80:5-6, May 10, 1962; 5-6 May 24, 1962. M-145.

Meyer, C.S., Vatican Council II addresses
protestantism, Concordia 38:77-89, Feb 1967. M-146.

Middleton, N., A layman's thoughts on the coming
Council, Clergy Rev 47:349-58, June 1962. M-147.

Miller, D., The future of Catholic schools,
Liguorian 54:115-20, May 1966. M-148.

Miller, D., Virtues for Catholics in a time of
change, Liguorian 56:27-31, Dec 1968. M-149.

Miller, D., What does freedom of conscience mean?
Liguorian 54:10-15, July 1966. M-150.

Miller, J., Mediator Dei and Vatican II on the
liturgy, Priest 21:822-6, Oct 1965. M-151.

Miller, J., The parish priest and the liturgical
movement, Liturgy 33:25-31, April 1964. M-152.

Miller, John M., ed. Vatican II: an interfaith
appraisal, 1966 Notre Dame, $12.50. M-153.

Miller, L., Vatican II: newsmakers and news-
writers, Liguorian 52:34-8, Feb 1964. M-154.

Miller, R.J., All roads lead to Rome in 1961,
Liguorian 47:1-6, Sept 1959. M-155.

Miller, R., Rainbow over the Vatican: contrast
between the two Vatican Councils, Liguorian
51:37-41, March 1963. M-156.

Mind of its own: third session, Time 84:75,
Nov 20, 1964. M-157.

Minear, P., Vatican II and Church renewal: Quo
Vadis? 1965 Yale. M-158.

Missionary meaning of the General Council, Shield
41:6 Jan 1962. M-159.

Missions and Council, America 106:712,
March 3, 1962.   M-160.

Misunderstanding still, America 109:128, Aug 10,
1963.   M-161.

Mixed marriage obstacle, America 111:282,
Sept 19, 1964.   M-162.

Mixed marriages and the Council: Fr. Haring's
article. Tablet 216:819, Sept 1, 1962.   M-163.

Moats, A. L. , Some of the Pope's problems, Nat
Rev 17:367, May 4, 1965.   M-164.

Modern means of communication, Extensn 59:26,
Jan 1965.   M-165.

Moeller, C. , The Church in the modern world,
Lumen 21:291-306, Sept 1966.   M-166.

Moeller, C. , The conciliar declaration on non-
christian religions and the decree on ecumenism,
Lumen 21:506-28, Dec 1966.   M-167.

Moeller, C. , Postconciliar perspectives in theology
and catechesis, Lumen 22:105-23, March 1967.   M-168.

Mole, J. , The communications decree of the second
Vatican Council, Soc Just 59:274-340, Dec 1966.   M-169.

Mollinari, P. , The following of Christ in the teaching
of Vatican II, Way suppl 4, 92-119, Nov 1967.   M-170.

Moments for memories, Sign 43:34-9, Oct 1963.   M-171.

Monsignor nods; Fr Bandas and criticism of communications media draft, America 110:357,
March 21, 1964.   M-172.

Montini, G. , Aims of Second Vatican Council,
Tablet 214:788, Aug 27, 1960.   M-173.

Montini, G. , The Church, 1964, Helicon. $5.50.   M-174.

Mood for the Council, America 113:278, Sept 18,
1965.   M-175.

Moody, J., Vatican II and the episcopacy, Hom
  Past Rev 66:22-32, Oct 1965.   M-176.

Mooney, L., A fireside view, Scapular 23:26-8,
  June 1964.   M-177.

Moore, A.J., Vatican II: session four, Christianity
  & Cr 25:245-6, Nov 15, 1965.   M-178.

Moorman, J., An Anglican observer looks at the
  schema on the liturgy. Thomist 27:440-50, April-
  July-Oct 1963.   M-179.

Moorman, J., Catholic Secretariat for relations with
  Non-Christians inadvisable according to Anglican
  observer, Unitas 15:304-5, Winter 1963.   M-180.

Moorman, J., Dialogue with non-Christians may
  side-tract unity efforts, Cath Mssngr 81:7,
  Oct 24, 1963.   M-181.

Moorman, J., The Pope would head a united Church,
  Tablet 217:1158, Oct 26, 1963.   M-182.

Moorman, J.R.H., Vatican Observed, 1967 Darton.   M-183.

Moran, G., The Theology of Revelation, 1966
  Herder and Herder, $4.95.   M-183a.

Moran, W., Population problem faces Council, Cath
  Mssngr 81:12, Oct 3, 1963.   M-184.

Morawaka, A., Secular awareness and the dark night
  of the Church, Cross Curr. 18:34-40, Winter
  1968.   M-185.

More cooperation: committee for religious, America
  112:183-4, Feb 6, 1965.   M-186.

More iron curtain bishops, Tablet 216:995, Oct 20,
  1962.   M-187.

More major changes in Catholic beliefs, US News
  59:12, Nov 8, 1965.   M-188.

More observers for Council named; no Jewish
observer after all, Tablet 216:773, Aug 18, 1962. M-189.

More observers named; uncertainty over Greek observers, Tablet 216:970, Oct 13, 1962. M-190.

Morgenthau, H. , The Jewish declaration, Commonweal 83:142-4, Nov 5, 1965; Replies 295, Dec 10,
1965. M-191.

Moscow, patriarch gives views on Second Vatican
Council, Unitas 15:62-3, Spring 1963. M-192.

Moscow Patriarchate and the Council, Tablet
216:843, Sept 8, 1962. M-193.

Moss, R. V. , Ecumenical implications of the Second
Vatican Council, Theol & Life 7:270-9, Winter
1964. M-194.

Most universal Council in church history; statistics
of responses to the Pope's invitation, Cath Mssngr
80:5, Feb 15, 1962. M-195.

Most, W. G. , Guide to renewal for teachers of
sacred doctrine, Cath Educ Rev 66:217-229,
April 1968. M-196.

Motter, A. , Protestant leader lauds Council results,
Unitas 18:61-2, Spring 1966. M-197.

Mueller, F. , The Parish of the future, Past Life
25:133-46, March 1967. M-198.

Muench, M. , and Ahlbrecht, A. , An ecumenical
house on the Council's periphery, Am Bene Rev
15:198-205, June 1964. M-199.

Muldoon, P. , Constitution on the liturgy, its scope
and emphasis, Irish Eccl Rev 101:182-4, March
1964. M-200.

Muldoon, P. , Instruction on the liturgical formation
of seminarians, Irish Eccl Rev 105:105-9, Feb
1966. M-201.

Muldoon, P., Vatican Council II: constitution on
the liturgy, Irish Eccl Rev 101:101-5, Feb 1964.　M-202.

Mullen, M., Decree on media of social communication, Cath Educ 34:600, Feb 1964.　M-203.

Muller, F.J., The day before, Friar 14:5-10,
Aug 1960.　M-204.

Mullin, J., The young Churches at the Council;
adaptation and world evangelization, Tablet
218:1282-3, Nov 14, 1964.　M-205.

Mumford, L., Bringing the Council home to
Germany, Herder 4:39-44, Feb 1967.　M-206.

Murphy, F.X., American bishops and the Council,
Extensn 57:27, Nov 1962.　M-207.

Murphy, F.X., The Church in the space age,
Extensn 57:12, Oct 1962.　M-208.

Murphy, F.X., The Council opens; several major
questions of divergent opinions, America 107:925-
28, Oct 20, 1962.　M-209.

Murphy, F.X.,The decree on priestly formation, Hom
Past Rev 66:283-9, Jan 1966.　M-210.

Murphy, F.X., The Ecumenical Council, Extensn
57:4, Dec 1962.　M-211.

Murphy, F.X.,The first historians of the Second Vatican
Council, Cath Hist Rev 49:540-47, Jan 1964.　M-212.

Murphy, F.X., New Constitution on the Church, Cath
Wrld 200:346-53, March 1965.　M-213.

Murphy, F.X., Our great Vatican Council: a preview, Sign 40:9, July 1961.　M-214.

Murphy, F.X., The politique of the Council; Vatican
II's first session, America 107:1248-51, Dec 15,
1962.　M-215.

Murphy, F. X. , II Vatican Council's constitution on
the sacred liturgy, Australian Cath Record
41:57-74, Jan 1964.   M-216.

Murphy, F. X. , Secrecy at the Council, America
109-96-7, July 27, 1963.   M-217.

Murphy, F. , Vatican II: early appraisal, America
108:330-2, March 9, 1963.   M-218.

Murphy, F. , Vatican II needs a new approach; in-
adequacy of scholastic methodology, Cath Wrld
198:302-7, Feb 1964.   M-219.

Murphy, G. , Charisms and Church Renewal, 1965,
Rome, Cath Book Agency, Thesis.   M-220.

Murphy, J. L. , Second Vatican Council: basic background information, Cath Sch J 62:33-36, Sept
1962.   M-221.

Murphy, M. J. , Presidential address, Cath Theol
Soc of Am Proceedings 14:185-92, 1969.   M-222.

Murray, G. , The translation of De Ecclesia, Tablet
219:583-4; Replies: 612, May 29; 668-9, June 12;
725, July 26; 1305-6, Nov 20; 1333-4, Nov 27;
1365-6, Dec 4, 1965.   M-223.

Murray, J. , Beneficial delay on religious liberty;
Tablet 218:1447-8, Dec 19, 1964.   M-224.

Murray, J. C. , The Church and the Council, America
109:451-3, Oct 19, 1963.   M-225.

Murray, J. , The declaration on religious freedom:
its deeper significance, America 114:592-3,
April 23, 1966.   M-226.

Murray, J. , ed. Freedom and Man, 1965 Kenedy.
$3. 95.   M-227.

Murray, J. , Freedom, authority, community, America
115:734-7, Dec 3, 1966.   M-228.

Murray, J., The issue of Church and state at Vatican
II, Theol Stds 27:580-606, Dec 1966.   M-229.
Murray, J., On religious liberty; relatio of Bp. De
Smedt and text on religious freedom, America
109:704-6, Nov 30, 1964.   M-230.
Murray, J., Religious Liberty: An End and a Be-
ginning, 1966 Macmillan, $4.95.   M-231.
Murray, J., Religious liberty and the development
of doctrine, Cath Wrld, 204:277-83, Feb 1967.   M-232.
Murray, J., This matter of religious freedom,
America 112:40-3, Jan 9, 1965.   M-233.
Murray, R., New Testament eschatology and the
constitution De Ecclesia, Heythrop 7:33-42,
Jan 1966.   M-234.
Must the Council end? Commonweal 80:3-4, March 27,
1964.   M-235.
Myers, R., The Council's call to change, Dominicana
49:142-8, Summer 1964.   M-236.

Nabaa, P., The Council and Christian unity, Unitas
14:92-104, Summer 1962; 186-200, Fall 1962.   N-1.
National Catholic Welfare Conf., Council Daybook,
1965 N.C.W.C., $22.50, 4 vols.   N-2.
NCWC: new life and vigor, America 115:643,
Nov 19, 1966.   N-3.
National Conference of Christians and Jews, Second
Vatican Council - its meaning for mankind, 1964
the Conference, $.10.   N-4.
National Conference of Christians and Jews, Vatican
II - fourth session, 1966 the Conference, $.50.   N-5.
Need for criticism, Commonweal 79:243, Nov 22,
1963.   N-6.

123

Nelson, C. D. , A Catholic-Protestant conversation,
America 106:186-89, Nov 11, 1961.   N-7.

Nelson, C. D. , Council preparations: a Protestant
view; Cath Wrld 194:144-49, Dec 1961.   N-8.

Nelson, C. D. , The Pope calls a Council, Christian
Cent. , 78:1136-8, 1172-4, Sept 27, Oct 4, 1961. N-9.

Nelson, C. D. , Protestant surveys schema thirteen:
The Church in the modern world, Cath Wrld
201:394-9, Sept 1965.   N-10.

Nelson, C. D. , Second Vatican Council, Relig in Life
32:69-79, Winter 1962-3.   N-11.

Nelson, C. D. , Second Vatican Council: a good beginning, Intl J of Relig Educ 39:2, March 1963.   N-12.

Nelson, C. D. , The Vatican Council and All
Christians, 1962 Assoc, $3.00.   N-13.

Nelson, J. R. , Romano, ma non troppo, Christian
Cent 83: June 29, 1966.   N-14.

Nelson, R. , A Methodist comment, Furrow 16:3-20,
Jan 1965.   N-15.

Nestorian observers, Tablet 218:1067, Sept 19, 1964. N-16.

Neville, R. , Genial Pope, Sat Eve Post 235:17-21,
Oct 6, 1962.   N-17.

Neville, R. , Pope John's plans for the Church, Sat
Eve Post 235:22-5, Oct 13, 1962.   N-18.

Neville, R. , Pope Paul follows along Pope John's
path, NY Times Mag p. 23, Sept 22, 1963.   N-19.

Nevins, A. , Christian vocation is to share, not to
hoard Christ's redemption, Cath Mssngr 83:15,
Dec 19, 1964.   N-20.

New churches for old; the architectural implications
of the liturgy decree, Tablet 218:180-81, Feb 15,
1964, Replies 248-49, Feb 29, 1964, 304,

124

March 14, 1964, Rejoinder 332, March 21, 1964. N-21.

New era in the Catholic Church, US News 55:100,
    Dec 16, 1963. N-22.

New Greek observers at third session, Tablet
    218:1212, Oct 24, 1964. N-23.

New image for the Catholic Church, US News
    55:112, Nov 25, 1963. N-24.

New revisions on the declaration on the Jews,
    America 113:430, Oct 16, 1965. N-25.

A New spring, Soc Just 56:303, Jan 1964. N-26.

New York Times Index

1961:838-40	1963:667-8	1966:970-2
855-6	681-3	1020
1962:780-2	1964:875-6	1967:1020
798-9	894-6	
	1965:809-11	
	832-3	N-27.

The New Yorker on the Council, Priest 18:1025-30,
    Dec 1962. N-28.

News coverage of Vatican II: Bosler, Elson, Fey,
    Hollis, Reedy, Zuroweste, Critic 21:53-8,
    March 1963. N-29.

Nicholas, J., Ecumenical aspects of the confession
    of 1967, Ecumenist 6:107-10, Nov-Dec 1967. N-30.

Niebuhr, Reinhold, After the second session, New
    Leader 47:11-12, Jan 20, 1964. N-31.

Niebuhr, R., Drama of the Vatican Council
    Christianity & Cr 24:275-8, Jan 11, 1965. N-32.

Niebuhr, R., Further reactions to Vatican II,
    Christianity & Cr 23:259-60, Jan 20, 1964. N-33.

Nine lay leaders suggest more ideas for Vatican
    Council, Sign 41:14-15, Oct 1961. N-34.

Nissiotis, N. A., Ecclesiology and ecumenism of the
second session of Vatican Council II, Gk Orth
Theol R 10 1:15-36, 1964.   N-35.
Nissiotis, N. A., Is the Vatican Council really
ecumenical? Ecum Rev 16:357-77, July 1964.   N-36.
Nissiotis, N. A., Main ecclesiological problem of
the Second Vatican Council and the position of
the non-Roman Churches facing it, J Ecum Studies
2:31-62, Winter 1965.   N-37.
Nissiotis, N. A., Orthodox reflections on the decree
on ecumenism, J Ecum Studies 3:329-42, Spring
1966.   N-38.
Nissiotis, N. A., Report on the Second Vatican
Council, Ecum Rev 18:190-206, April 1966.   N-39.
Nissuitusm, B., Council called "pan Roman Synod"
by Orthodox observer for WCC; Cath Mssngr
82:9, July 23, 1964.   N-40.
No comment at Hartford; the National Council of
Churches, America 100:674, March 14, 1959.   N-41.
No miracles from the Council, Tablet 215:66,
Jan 21, 1961.   N-42.
No new definitions, please; Prof. Hirschmann's
address, Tablet 216:628, June 30, 1962.   N-43.
No observers from Athens or Constantinople, Tablet
217:803, July 20, 1963.   N-44.
No turning back, America 108:852-3, June 15, 1963. N-45.
No venacular yet, Tablet 218:138, Feb 1, 1964.   N-46.
Non-Catholic influence: WCC conference in Montreal
will affect the Council, Ave 98:18, Aug 17, 1963. N-47.
Non-Christian observers and a non-Christian
Secretariat? Tablet 217:439-40, Aug 20, 1963.   N-48.

Noonan, J. T. , Contraception and the Council,
Commonweal 83:657-62, March 11, 1966.   N-49.

Norgen, W. , Thoughts of an observer, Lamp
62:14-15, Oct 1964.   N-50.

Norms for implementing the decree Ad Gentes of
the Second Vatican Council, Furrow 17:675-9,
Oct 1966.   N-51.

Norris, F. B. , Decree on Priestly Training, 1966
Paulist, pb. $. 75.   N-52.

Norris, F. , The Persons who save us. Natl Liturg
Week 25:20-24, 1964.   N-53.

Norris, J. , American lay auditor tells of warm
reception Cath Mssngr 81:7, Oct 10, 1963.   N-54.

Norris, J. J. , Reply to John Cogley, America
112:594, April 24, 1965.   N-55.

Norris, J. , U. S. layman tells of poverty, Cath
Mssngr 82:9, Nov 12, 1964.   N-56.

Northcott, C. , Boswell in St Peter's: D. Horton's
Vatican diary, Christian Cent 83:359, March 23,
1966.   N-57.

Northcott, C. , Punctures balloon words: Lukas
Vischer, observer at the Vatican Council,
Christian Cent 82:134, Feb 3, 1965.   N-58.

Norton-Taylor, D. , A Catholic layman confronts
his changing Church, Fortune 74:172-5, Dec 1966. N-59.

Note on schema 14, America 114:280, Feb 26, 1966. N-60.

Notre Dame Conference: Vatican II comes to America,
Ave 103:4, April 9, 1966.   N-61.

Notre Dame, Univ. , International Theological Conference: Vatican II, 1966 Notre Dame, $12. 50,
pb. $. 95.   N-62.

Novak, M. , Act one of the Vatican Council, New
Repub 148:15-17, Jan 12, 1963.   N-63.

Novak, M. , American Catholicism after the Council,
Commentary 40:50-8, August 1965.   N-64.

Novak, M. , The city of Rome prepares, Commonweal 76:463-64, Aug 24, 1962.   N-65.

Novak, M. , Coming Vatican Council, New Repub
147:12-14, Aug 27, 1962.   N-66.

Novak, M. , Ecumenical sadness and hope, Christian
Cent 81:1518, Dec 9, 1964.   N-67.

Novak, M. , Intrigue in the Council, New Repub
150:10-11, Jan 11, 1964.   N-68.

Novak, M. , The Open Church, 1964 Macmillan,
$6. 50.   N-69.

Novak, M. , Open Church: Vatican II, Act II, 1964
Macmillan, $6. 50.   N-70.

Novak, M. , Pope Paul's address to the curia,
Commonweal 79:89-90, Oct 18, 1963.   N-71.

Novak, M. , Rome isn't covered in a day, Critic
22:39-43, June 1964.   N-72.

Novak, M. , Vatican II, Act III, New Repub
151:7-8, Oct 17, 1964.   N-73.

Novak, M. , When is doctrine pure? Commonweal
80:233-5, May 15, 1964.   N-74.

Novak, M. , Will the Council build the bridge? US
Cath 90:9-13, Oct 1964.   N-75.

Novak, M. , Winds of change in Rome, New Repub
149:11-3, Nov 16, 1963.   N-76.

Nowell, R. , The ecumenical decree, Tablet
218:1162-3, Oct 17, 1963.   N-77.

Nowell, R. , Martyrs and patriarchs, Tablet
218:1194-6, Oct 24, 1964.   N-78.

Nowell, R., What is the world? schema 13,
Tablet 218:1221-2, Oct 31, 1964.   N-79.

Number of African-born bishops at Council in-
creased, Shield 43:12, Dec-Jan 1963, 1964.   N-80.

Oberman, H.A., Interview with Dr. Heiko Oberman,
Protestant observer, Cath Wrld 197:100-6,
May 1963.   O-1.

Oberman, H.A., Lonely Pope or first of the
brethren? Christian Cent 82:835-7, June 30, 1965. O-2.

O'Boyle, Card., Racism and the Council, America
111:647, Nov 21, 1964.   O-3.

O'Brien, D., Patriarch of Moscow and the Council,
Blkfrs 42:474-76, Nov 1961.   O-4.

O'Brien, E., The Council and reunion; Month
27:15-19, Jan 1962.   O-5.

O'Brien, E., Reform in the Church; Commonweal
75:664-66, March 23, 1962.   O-6.

O'Brien, J.A., Catching Up with the Church, 1967,
Herder and Herder, $4.50.   O-7.

O'Brien, J., Melkite Patriarch Maximos IV: giant
of the Council, Past Life 26:369-74, June 1968.   O-8.

O'Brien, W.V., After nineteen years: let us begin,
Wrldview 7:4-15, Dec 1964.   O-9.

O'Brien, W., Morality, nuclear war, and the schema
on the Church in the modern world, Cath Assoc
for Intl Peace News 25:6-8, Oct 1964.   O-10.

O'Brien, W.V., War and peace and the American
Catholic, Cath Wrld 202:331-5, March 1966.   O-11.

Observer appointed Rev T. Abraham of the Jacobite
Church, Cath Mssngr 82:12, Aug 13, 1964.   O-12.

The observers, Tablet 219:1071-2, Sept 25, 1965.   O-13.

The observers at the Council; Eastern Churches
Q 15:92-8, Fall 1963.   O-14.

Observers for the Council; list, Tablet 216:868,
Sept 15, 1962.   O-15.

Observers for the third session, Tablet 218:955,
Aug 22, 1964.   O-16.

Observers from Constantinople, Tablet 218:1067,
Sept 19, 1964.   O-17.

Observers represent 21 Churches; third session,
Cath Mssngr 82:9, Sept 24, 1964.   O-18.

O'Callaghan, D. , Sacraments of faith; Vatican II's
constitution on the liturgy, Irish Eccl Rev
101:333-8, May 1964.   O-19.

O'Carroll, M. , The Council, Irish Eccl Rev
97:155-63. March 1962.   O-20.

O'Collins, G. , Divine revelation, Month 35:332-6,
June 1966.   O-21.

O'Connell, J. , The new instruction on the liturgy,
Clergy Rev 52:702-5, Sept 1967.   O-22.

O'Connell, J. , The new constitution on the sacred
liturgy, Clergy Rev 49:65-9, Feb 1964.   O-23.

O'Connell, J. , The new constitution on the sacred
liturgy, Priest 20:311-15, April 1964.   O-24.

O'Connor, E. , Vatican II and the renewal of religious,
Rev Relig 26:404-23, May 1967.   O-25.

O'Connor, J. , Council should canonize Pope John
by acclamation, Furrow 15:544-5, Aug 1964.   O-26.

O'Connor, J. , Vatican Council should canonize Pope
John; reply, Wiseman 238:261, Fall 1964.   O-27.

O'Dea, T. F. , The Catholic Crisis, 1968 Beacon,
$ 5. 95.   O-28.

O'Donnell, R. , Council's first session in retrospect, Cath Layman 77:9-16, Feb 1963. O-29.

O'Donnell, T. , Ecumenical character of the Second
Vatican Council, Studies 51:337-48, Autumn 1962. O-30.

O'Donoghue, J. , Elections in the Church, Commonweal 82:281-3, May 21, 1965. O-31.

O'Donohoe, J. , Vatican II and seminary reform,
Priest 23:281-8, April 1967. O-32.

Oecumenical character of the Second Vatican
Council, Studies 51:337-48, Fall 1962. O-33.

Oesterreicher, J. , Christians and Jews and a
conciliar declaration, Month 33:221-30, April
1965. O-34.

Oesterreicher, J. , The Church and the non-Christian
world; man's many religions, Hom Past Rev
66:478-86, March 1966. O-35.

Oesterreicher, J. , A Jewish Christian scholar looks
at the Conciliar statement on Jews, US Cath
31:21-9, Feb 1966. O-36.

Oesterreicher, J. M. , Reply to G. A. Lindbeck,
Christianity & Cr 26:133, June 13, 1966. O-37.

Oesterreicher, J. , Statement on Jews purely
pastoral, Cath Mssngr 82:8, May 14, 1964. O-38.

Oesterreicher, J. , Why Judaism and Old Testament
should be dealt with by Council, Cath Mssngr
82:9, Dec 5, 1963. O-39.

O'Flynn, J. , The constitution on divine revelation,
Irish Theol Q 33:254-65, July 1966. O-40.

O'Flynn, J. , The inspirations of Scripture, Irish
Eccl Rev 107:362-73, June 1967. O-41.

O'Gara, J. , Council post-mortem, Commonweal
79:569, Feb 7, 1964. O-42.

O'Gara, J., Council revisited, Commonweal
    81:258-9, Nov 20, 1964.   O-43.

O'Gara, J., End of the session, Commonweal
    81:373-5, Dec 11, 1964.   O-44.

O'Gara, J., The Jewish declaration, Commonweal
    83:332, Dec 17, 1965.   O-45.

O'Gara, J., Layman's hopes, Commonweal 81:87,
    Oct 16, 1964.   O-46.

O'Gara, J., Meanwhile, back at home; unreadiness
    for changes, Commonweal 79:216, Nov 15, 1963. O-47.

O'Gara, J., Notre Dame Conference; International
    conference on the theological issues of Vatican
    II, Commonweal 84:98, April 15, 1966.   O-48.

O'Gara, J., Report from Rome, Commonweal
    79:157-8, Nov 1, 1963.   O-49.

O'Gorman, K., Sacred music; commentary on
    chapter 6 of the Vatican Council II constitution
    on the liturgy, Doctrine & Life 14:123-6, Feb
    1964.   O-50.

O'Gorman, N., Opening the Council, Jubilee
    10:10-12, Dec 1962.   O-51.

O'Grady, D., The evolving Church, Tablet
    222:1110-2, Nov 9, 1968.   O-52.

O'Grady, D., Humor from Vatican II, Ave 102:7-8,
    Dec 25, 1965.   O-53.

O'Grady, D., Schema 13: the Church in the modern
    world, US Cath 31:19-20, Nov 1965.   O-54.

O'Grady, D., That was the Council that was, US
    Cath 31:50-53, Jan 1966.   O-55.

O'Grady, D., Towards a Church of the poor,
    Perspectives 10:36-44, March-April 1965.   O-56.

O'Hanlon, D. J. and Campion, D. R., Council
jottings, America 109:341-3; 377-8; 409-10;
446-7; 508-510; 553-5; 626-7; 701-2; 765-6;
791, Sept 28 - Dec 21, 1963.   O-57.

O'Hanlon, D. J., Dialogue at the top, America
109:231-4, Sept 7, 1963. Reply: D. A. Walsh,
109:441, Oct 19, 1963.   O-58.

O'Hanlon, D. J., Vatican II: a look ahead, America
109:347-9, Sept 28, 1963.   O-59.

O'Hara, G. P., Cardinal Bea: an appreciation,
America 108:442-4, March 30, 1963.   O-60.

O'Hara, J. M., French Canada and the Council;
summary of laymen's views, Thought 37:325-29,
Fall 1962.   O-61.

O'Keefe, P. E., Reporting session four, America
113:19, July 3, 1965.   O-62.

Olsen, A. L., Constitution on divine revelation,
Dialog 5:182-7, Summer 1966.   O-63.

On changes in the Church, America 113:150,
Aug 14, 1965.   O-64.

On Implementing the Council, Commonweal
84:516, Aug 19, 1966.   O-65.

On peace and war; need for statement by the
Council, Commonweal 77:449, Jan 25, 1963.   O-66.

On the Jews: reprint from the Pilot, US Cath
30:56, July 1964.   O-67.

Onclin, W., Decree on the Pastoral Office of
Bishops in the Church, 1967 Paulist, pb $1. 45.   O-68.

O'Neill, C., Concessions for unity, Doctrine & Life
14:583-95, Dec 1964.   O-69.

O'Neill, C. A., ed. Ecumenism and Vatican II,
1964 Bruce, $3. 75.   O-70.

O'Neill, C., The first session, Doctrine & Life
13:4-14, Jan 1963.   O-71.

O'Neill, J., Lay apostolate schema rapped;
Orthodox intercommunion okayed, Cath Mssngr
82:11, Oct 15, 1964.   O-72.

O'Neill, J., Predicts 3rd session most productive,
Cath Mssngr 82:1, July 30, 1964.   O-73.

O'Neill, J., U.S., Canadian bishops to report on
Council via taped interviews, Cath Mssngr 82:9,
Sept 10, 1964.   O-74.

Only three bishops from Czechoslovakia at Council's
second session, Tablet 217:1048, Sept 28, 1963.   O-75.

Opening ceremonies of the second session, Illus
Lond News 243:501, Oct 5, 1963.   O-76.

Options at the fourth session, Christian Cent
82:1147, Sept 22, 1965.   O-77.

Organization of Council changed; Cardinal moderators,
new Secretariat, Tablet 217:1019, Sept 21, 1963. O-78.

O'Riodan, S., Looking towards the second session;
the schemata, Furrow 14:607-16, Oct 1963.   O-79.

O'Riordan, S., Pope, Curia and the bishops, Guide
185:3-8, Feb 1964.   O-80.

O'Riordan, S., The third session, Furrow
15:621-8, Oct 1964, 685-94, Nov 1964, 762-74,
Dec 1964.   O-81.

O'Riordan, S., Will Vatican II really change the
Church, Liguorian 53:2-7, June 1966.   O-82.

O'Rourke, K., New laws for religious, Cross &
Crown 19:12-22, March 1967.   O-83.

Orsy, L.M., Decree on religious life, America
114:12-13, Jan 1, 1966.   O-84.

Orsy, L., Quantity and quality of laws after
Vatican II, Jurist 27:385-412, Oct 1967.   O-85.

Orsy, L., Vatican II and the revision of canon law,
Clergy Rev 53:83-100, Feb 1968.   O-86.

Orthodox and unity, America 107:1203, Dec 8, 1965.   O-87.

Orthodox Church confirms World Council loyalty,
Christian Cent 76:605, May 20, 1959.   O-88.

Orthodox divergences, Tablet 216:339-40, April 7,
1962.   O-89.

Orthodox look to Geneva rather than Rome,
Christian Cent 76:1173-4, Oct 14, 1959.   O-90.

Orthodox observers seen still possible, Cath Mssngr
81:20, Dec 20, 1962.   O-91.

Orthodox Patriarch of Alexandria condemns De
Iudaeis, Tablet 218:1421, Dec 12, 1964.   O-92.

Osborne, W., Catholic Church reform in the United
States too late? Dominicans 52:4-14, Spring 1967.   O-93.

O'Shea, C. F., The Secretariat for promoting
Christian unity, At-one-ment 4:140-5, 1962.   O-94.

Osterhaven, M. E., New Catholicism and the Bible,
Reformed Rev 21:54-9, Sept 1967.   O-95.

O'Sullivan, D., Sacred art; commentary on chapter
7 of the Vatican Council II constitution on the
liturgy, Doctrine & Life 14:126-9, Feb 1964.   O-96.

Otilio, Fr., St. Theresa of Jesus and of the Council,
Spir Life 2:4-16, Spring 1965.   O-97.

Ottaviani, A., Errors and dangers; letter to the
bishops, Tablet 220:1168-9, Oct 15, 1966.
Replies: Oct 22, 1966.   O-98.

Ottaviani, A., Letter... on strange and audacious
opinions, Christ to the Wrld 12:65-7, Jan 1967.
Reply: 157:65, March-April 1967.   O-99.

Ottensmeyer, H., The Council and the seminary,
Priest 22:988-93, Dec 1966. O-100.

Our brethren's prayers; cases of Protestants'
prayers for success, America 107:830-31,
Oct 6, 1962. O-101.

Our man at the Vatican, Tablet 220:894, Aug 6,
1966. O-102.

Outler, A. C., Council, one year later, Commonweal 85:368-72, Jan 6, 1967. O-103.

Outler, A. C., Methodist Observer at Vatican II,
1967, Newman, $4.50. O-104.

Outler, A. C., Reflections of a Council observer,
Cath Wrld 203:353-60, Sept 1966. O-105.

Outler, A. C., Reformation Roman style, Frontier
9:9-13, Spring 1966, Cath Wrld 204:341-5,
March 1967. O-106.

Outler, A. C., Vatican II: a synoptic view, Lond
Q & HR 102:188-99, July 1967. O-107.

Outler, A. C., Vatican II: act three, Christianity
& Cr 24:260-4, Dec 28, 1964. O-108.

Overath, J., Church music in the light of the constitution on the liturgy, Sacred Music 92:3-11,
Winter 1965. O-109.

Palms, C., Development of doctrine, Cath Wrld
202:324, March 1966. P-1.

Palms, C., The impact of the Council, Cath Wrld
201:349-50, Sept 1965. P-2.

Palms, C., Leading figures at the Council; Cards
R. Silva Henriquez, A. Bea, B. Alfrink and
others, Cath Wrld 195:200-09, July 1962. P-3.

Pan-Africa at Vatican II, America 107:972, Nov 3,
1962. P-4.

136

Parish priests at the Council, Tablet 218:1182,
   Oct 17, 1964.   P-5.

Parochial schools still the answer, America
   113:516-7, Nov 6, 1965.   P-6.

Pastor Boigner's big four; issues of Protestant
   interest, Tablet 216:628, June 20, 1962.   P-7.

Pastoral constitution, see Constitution C-178.   P-8.

The pastoral role of bishops, Extensn 59:28,
   Jan 1965.   P-9.

Patience and the Council, America 112:279-80,
   Feb 27, 1965.   P-10.

Paton, D. M., New Delhi and Rome: the Vatican
   Council and non-Roman Churches, Mod Chm
   6:69-79, Oct 1962.   P-11.

Paul and the curia, Newsweek 62:62, Sept 30, 1963. P-12.

Paul VI, Pope, see also: Montini, Giovanni.   P-13.

Paul VI, Pope, Closing address- fourth session,
   Vatican Council II, 1966 N.C.W.C., $.35.   P-14.

Paul VI, Pope, Ecumenical Council address,
   Sept 14, 1964, Vital Speeches 30:738-40, Oct 1,
   1964.   P-15.

Paul VI, Pope, Ecumenical Council, address
   Sept 15, 1965, Vital Speeches 31:738-41, Oct 1,
   1965.   P-16.

Paul VI, Pope, Organization of the second session
   of the 2nd Vatican Council, The Pope Speaks
   9:146-9, 1964.   P-17.

Paul VI, Pope, Papal brief declaring the Council
   completed. Latin text AAS 58:18-19, Jan 31, 1966. P-18.

Paul VI, Pope, Post duos menses; on the conclusion
   of the third session of the 2nd Vatican Council,
   Tablet 218:1353-4, Nov 28, 1964.   P-19.

Paul VI, Pope, Religious value of the Council,
Cath Wrld 203:113-14, May 1966.   P-20.

Paul VI, Pope, Sacram liturgiam; motu proprio
implementing the liturgical constitution, Tablet
218:150-51, Feb 8, 1964.   P-21.

Paul VI, Pope, Second Vatican Council, closing
address, second session, 1963, N.C.W., $.25.   P-22.

Paul VI, Pope, To the Sacred College of Cardinals
on the feast day of the Pope: the Council...
summarized, The Pope Speaks 12:203-10 #3,
1967.   P-23.

Paul VI, Pope, Writings and speeches, The Pope
Speaks, vols 9-13.   P-24.

Pawley, B.C., An Anglican View of the Vatican
Council, 1962 Morehouse, $2.90.   P-25.

Pawley, B.C., ed. Second Vatican Council: Studies
by Eight Anglican Observers, 1967 Oxford, pb
$3.75.   P-26.

Pawley, B., Vatican observer, Jubilee 10:16-7,
March 1963.   P-27.

Peerman, D., Balancing act, Christian Cent
82:1534-5, Dec 15, 1965.   P-28.

Pelikan, J., That the Church may be more fully
Catholic, Cath Wrld 198:151-6, Dec 1963.   P-29.

Pellegrino, M., Nova et vetera, Furrow 19:495-515,
Sept 1968.   P-30.

Pellegrino, M., The priest and the intellectual life,
Furrow 17:265-8, April 1966.   P-31.

Penance for the Council; Card Godfrey's pastoral,
Tablet 216:774, Aug 18, 1962.   P-32.

Pennington, M., The structure of the section concerning religious life in the revised code, Jurist

25:271-90, July 1965.   P-33.

Pennington, M., Vatican II and the comtemplative
   life, Hom Past Rev 67:566-7, March 1967.   P-34.

Pentecost and the Council; beseeching the aid of
   the Holy Spirit, America 107:373, June 9, 1962.   P-35.

Pepper, C. G., Freud and man in Rome, Newsweek
   66:95, Oct 11, 1965.   P-36.

Perennes, H., Our Lady and the modern Church,
   Marist 20:7-10, May-June 1964.   P-37.

Permanent preparatory commission? Tablet
   215:1192, Dec 9, 1961.   P-38.

Perplexed Pope, Economist 215:746, May 15, 1965.   P-39.

Persich, N., Inside the Council, Jubilee 10:12-15,
   April 1963.   P-40.

Pessimists' guide to the Vatican Council, Ramparts
   4:20-34, Oct 1965.   P-41.

Peters, K., Catholics and anti-Semitism, Ave
   98:18, Oct 12, 1963.   P-42.

Peters, K. W., The Council and the Christian
   message, Ave 96:18, Dec 22, 1962.   P-43.

Petterson, A., A Presbyterian comment, Furrow
   16:3-20, Jan 1965.   P-44.

Petty, M., The Council on education, Cath Educ
   37:89-90, March 1967.   P-45.

Pfister, P., Missionary prospects for the Ecumenical
   Council, Japan Missionary Bulletin 15:368-71,
   July 1961.   P-46.

Phillips, A., Applying the Council in Australia,
   Tablet 221:200-2, Feb 25, 1967.   P-47.

Pierini, Franco, Catechism of Vatican II, 1967
   Alba, $4.95.   P-48.

Pierre, Sr., Reflections on article two of the
constitution, Worship 39:349-55, June 1965.   P-49.
The pilgrim and the Council, Ave 99:17, Jan 25,
1964.   P-50.
Piser, R., First session of the Council, Am Bene
Rev 14:240-7, June 1963.   P-51.
Piser, R., Great Council shines in Rome, Life
53:26-33, Nov 2, 1962.   P-52.
A place of honor for the Patriarchs, Tablet
217:1130, Oct 19, 1963.   P-53.
The place of Mary, Commonweal 79:212-13,
Nov 15, 1963, 81:29-30, Oct 2, 1964.   P-54.
Placet! Christian Cent 82:1563-4, Dec 22, 1965.   P-55.
Poelman, R., Adaptation of the choir in a Church,
Lumen 20:451-66, Sept 1965.   P-56.
Polish bishops' letter on Council tells scope and
purpose of event, Cath Mssngr 80:7, Feb 8, 1962. P-57.
Polish, D., Statement on the Jews; an inadequate
document, Christian Cent 82:1475-7, Dec 1,
1965. Reply: A.B. Williams 83:84-5, Jan 19,
1966.   P-58.
Polish hierarchy and the Council; joint pastoral,
Tablet 216:164, Feb 17, 1962.   P-59.
Polish voices at the Council; summary of Herder-K
report, Cross Currents 12:511-12, Fall 1962.   P-60.
Poncins, L., Judaism and the Vatican, 1967
Britons, 30s.   P-61.
The Pope and the bishops, Tablet 217:1347-8,
Dec 14, 1963.   P-62.
The Pope and the commissions: satisfactory con-
clusions, Tablet 216:363, April 14, 1962.   P-63.
The Pope and the Council, Blkfrs 40:99, Mar 1959.   P-64.

The Pope calls a Council, Commonweal 69:484,
  Feb 6, 1959.   P-65.
The Pope calls the Second Vatican Council,
  Christian Cent 79:76, Jan 17, 1962.   P-66.
Pope, Council and Jews, America 108:427,
  March 30, 1963.   P-67.
Pope in Council; the extraordinary magisterium
  and the revelation schema debate, Tablet
  216:1153-54, Dec 1, 1962.   P-68.
The Pope is clearly worried; warns of danger
  threatening Catholic orthodoxy, America 113:177,
  August 21, 1965.   P-69.
Pope John opens sessions of Ecumenical Council,
  Unitas 14:216-18, Fall 1962.   P-70.
Pope John receives Council observers in special
  audience, Unitas 14:218-19, Fall 1962.   P-71.
Pope John's announcement; Cath commentators
  Orthodox and Protestant reactions, Unitas
  11:57-61, Spring 1959.   P-72.
Pope John's great gift, Read Dgst 82:141-6, April
  1963.   P-73.
Pope John XXIII, Man of the year, Time 81:50-4,
  Jan 4, 1963; Discussion 81:10, Jan 18, 1963.   P-74.
Pope John XXIII plans a world Church Council,
  Christian Cent 76:363, March 25, 1959.   P-75.
Pope names preparatory commission for Ecumenical
  Council, Unitas 11:145, Summer 1959.   P-76.
Pope names press experts for Council, Editor and
  Publisher 94:28, Dec 9, 1961.   P-77.
Pope names 30 cardinals to revise code of canon
  law, Cath Mssngr 81:1, April 4, 1963.   P-78.

The Pope on the Council; summaries of documents
in chronological order, Doctrine and Life
11:547-58, Oct 1961; 603-05, Nov 1961.   P-79.

Pope opens second Council session, Christian Cent
80:1228, Oct 9, 1963.   P-80.

Pope Paul: liberal, conservative or compromiser?
US News 59:19, Sept 27, 1965.   P-81.

The Pope runs the Church, Time 84:66, Nov 27,
1964.   P-82.

The Pope sums up, Tablet 219:1410-11, Dec 18,
1965.   P-83.

The Pope's confidence in the Council, Ave 99:16,
May 2, 1964.   P-84.

Pope's keynote: synod of bishops, America 113:358,
Oct 2, 1965.   P-85.

Population and the Council, America 109:477,
Oct 26, 1963.   P-86.

Portasik, R., What has the Council done for me?
Friar 25:40-5, June 1966.   P-87.

Portman, J.R., The Concepts of Mission and Unity
in the World Council of Churches, 1966, Rome,
Catholic Book Agency, Thesis.   P-88.

Post-Council events, Cath Sch J 66:5, May 1966.   P-89.

Poulin, A., Reply to Hans Kung, Commonweal
83:76-7, Oct 22, 1965.   P-90.

Powell, J., Closed and/or open; liberal and conservative wrong terms to label Council Fathers,
America 109:484-6, Oct 26, 1963.   P-91.

Power, D., Vatican II and priestly formation,
Furrow 16:259-67, May 1965.   P-92.

Power struggle, Newsweek 60:59, Oct 29, 1962.   P-93.

Prayer for the General Council, Rev for Relig
    19:65, March 1960.   P-94.

Prayer used daily at the Council, Princeton Sem
    Bul 56:14, May 1963.   P-95.

Preaching the word of God, Natl Liturg Week
    25:217-20, 1964.   P-96.

Predicting the Council; mixed crosswinds of opinion.
    Commonweal 76:365, July 6, 1962.   P-97.

Preparation; appointments, Tablet 214:685-86,
    July 16, 1960.   P-98.

Preparation of the Council, Clergy M 25:340-43,
    Oct 1961.   P-99.

Preparing for the Council, Tablet 214:685-86,
    July 16, 1960.   P-100.

Preparing for the Council, Tablet 214:852,
    Sept 17, 1960.   P-101.

Preparing for the Council, Tablet 214:1076,
    Nov 19, 1960.   P-102.

Preparing for the Council, Tablet 215:368,
    April 15, 1961.   P-103.

Preparing for the Council: report on first five
    sessions of Central Prep. Commission, Tablet
    215:616, June 24, 1961.   P-104.

Preparing for the Ecumenical Council, Cath Mssngr
    79:7, Feb 23, 1961.   P-105.

Preparing for Vatican II, Doctrine and Life
    11:454-98, Sept 1961; 11:509-46, Oct 1961.   P-106.

Presbyter Anglicanus, Second Vatican Council: An
    Interim Report, 1963 Morehouse, $.95.   P-107.

Presbyterian views on the Vatican Council, Tablet
    217:899, Aug 17, 1963.   P-108.

Press and the Council; admirable coverage of
the first phase, America 107:1030, Nov 10, 1962. P-109.

Press at the Council, America 104:620-21,
Feb 11, 1961. P-110.

Press coverage at the Council; an unhappy portent,
Commonweal 76:509, Sept 21, 1962. P-111.

Press coverage satisfies worldwide Council interest,
Cath J 13:13-14, Nov 1962. P-112.

Press service for the Ecumenical Council, Tablet
215:1008, Oct 21, 1961. P-113.

Price, M., Briefing the press, Jubilee 13:16-9,
May 1965. P-114.

Price of freedom, America 112:513, April 17, 1965. P-115.

Primeau, E., Trends in liturgy and catechesis,
Am Bene Rev 17:273-83, Fall 1966. P-116.

Procedure modified for third session, Tablet
218:842, July 25, 1964. P-117.

Programme and rules for the third Council session,
Clergy M 28:313, Sept 1964. P-118.

Progress and a cloud, Commonweal 81:117,
Oct 23, 1964. P-119.

Progress at the Council, America 107:1080,
Nov 17, 1962. P-120.

Progress of plans, Hom Past Rev 61:974-75,
July 1961. P-121.

Progress since the Council, Cath Choirmaster
50:12, Spring 1964. P-122.

Progressives win, Economist 213:336, Oct 24, 1964. P-123.

Protest from Jordanian MP's Christians protest
attempt to clear Jews, Tablet 218:1184, Oct 17,
1964. P-124.

Protestant and Catholic leaders comment on
how should Vatican II be implemented? Ave
103:8-10, May 21, 1966.   P-125.

Protestant preview of Second Vatican Council,
Christianity Tdy 6:36-7, Sept 28, 1962.   P-126.

Protestants on the Council, America 108:288-9,
. March 2, 1963.   P-127.

Protestants to Rome, Time 80:38, Aug 24, 1962.   P-128.

Public image of the Catholic Church today, Cath
Wrld 199:352-5, Sept 1964.   P-129.

Publications on the constitution, Liturgy 33:74-5,
July 1964.   P-130.

Pujol, C., The conciliar decree on the Eastern
Catholic Churches, Unitas 17:28-41, Spring 1965. P-131.

Purdy, W., Appendix to enthusiasm: the Council and
the elect, Tablet 220:471-3, April 23, 1966.   P-132.

Purdy, W., The epitaph of clericalism, Tablet
220:93-4, Jan 22, 1966.   P-133.

Purdy, W., The Vatican Council: a retrospect,
Dublin Rev 240:17-33, Spring 1966.   P-134.

Purdy, W., Vatican II: the second session, Perspectives 9:36-51, March-April 1964.   P-135.

Puthiadam, I., The Council and the unity of
Christians according to Card. Bea, Clergy M
26:241-50, Aug 1962.   P-136.

Putting Council decrees into effect; remarks of
Abp. Palazzini, Cath Mssngr 81:1, Oct 17, 1963.   P-137.

Putz, L. J. Ecumenical Council; year end report,
Ave 96:4-5, Dec 29, 1962.   P-138.

Putz, J., First session of the Council, Clergy M
27:45-53, March 1963.   P-139.

Putz, L. , Keeping up with the Council; survey
of current books, Ave 98:14-15, Sept 14, 1963.   P-140.
Putz, J. , The Marian question, Clergy M
28:173-7, May 1964.   P-141.
A puzzlement: CPA award and sources of information for Council articles in New Yorker, Ave
97:16, May 1963.   P-142.

Quanbeck, W. , ed. Challenge and Response: A
Protestant Perspective of the Vatican Council,
1966 Augsburg, $5.00.   Q-1.
Quanbeck, W.A. , Dialog after the Council, Luth
Wrld 12 - 2:97-106, 1965.   Q-2.
Question of legality raised on collegiality, Cath
Mssngr 81:1, Oct 17, 1963.   Q-3.
Quinn, E. , Laymen and the Council, Tablet
215:362, April 15, 1961.   Q-4.

Racism and the Council, America 109:507, Nov 2,
1963; 111:647, Nov 21, 1964.   R-1.
Rahner, K. , Christian of the future, US Cath
31:13-8, Nov 1965.   R-2.
Rahner, K. , Church After the Council, 1967
Herder and Herder, $3.50.   R-3.
Ramsey, P. , Nuclear war and Vatican Council II,
Theol Tdy 23:244-63, July 1966.   R-4.
Ramsey, P. , The Vatican Council on modern war,
Theol Stds 27:179-203, June 1966.   R-5.
Rapp, U. , The constitution on the liturgy and
sacred art, Furrow 16:205-18, April 1965.   R-6.
Ratcliff, E.C. , Liturgy, the Second Vatican Council
and Life, Relig in Life 33:372-82, Summer 1964. R-7.

Ratzinger, J., Catholicism after the Council, Furrow 18:3-23, Jan 1967.   R-8.

Ratzinger, J., Second Vatican Council: the first session, Furrow 14:267-88, May 1963.   R-9.

Ratzinger, J., Theological Highlights of Vatican II, 1966 Paulist, $1.25.   R-10.

Reactionaries win the second round, Christian Cent 80:1568, Dec 18, 1963.   R-11.

Readiness for reform: second session's agenda, Time 82:82, Oct 4, 1963.   R-12.

Reading the Council documents, America 114:346-7, March 12, 1966.   R-13.

Realistic hope for Council: remarks of Card Bea. Ave 95:17, April 28, 1962.   R-14.

Reedy, J., Biggest news story in 1962, Ave 95:2, Jan 13, 1962   R-15.

Reedy, J., The human aspect of the Council, Ave 96:2, Oct 13, 1962.   R-16.

Reedy, J., Our obligation to pray for the Council, Ave 96:2, Oct 6, 1962.   R-17.

Reedy, J., TV coverage possibilities; humorous treatment, Ave 94:2, Dec 2, 1961.   R-18.

Re-examining Church structures; 4th session of the Central Prep Commission, Cath Mssngr 80:5-6, March 29, 1962.   R-19.

Reform and the liturgy; re-educating the people of God, Tablet 218:149-50, Feb 8, 1964.   R-20.

Regan, D., Brazil: a plan for recovery, Furrow 19:453-68, Aug 1968.   R-21.

Regan, P., Triumphalism, Cath Dgst 30:19-23, July 1966.   R-22.

Regan, R. J., Conflict and Consensus, 1967
    Macmillan, $5.95.   R-23.
Reid, J. K. S., Vatican Council II and the people of
    God, Ref & Presb Wrld 29, 12-22, March 1966.   R-24.
Reinhold, H. A., Liturgy and the Second Vatican
    Council: constitution on the sacred liturgy, Cath
    Wrld 198:347-56, March 1964.   R-25.
Reinhold, H., Vatican II: some unfinished business,
    Priest 20:1035-40, Dec 1964.   R-26.
Relations with non-Christians, America 113:490-1,
    Oct 30, 1965.   R-27.
Religion, morality and government; Vatican Council
    declaration for religious liberty, Tablet 218:1103-4,
    Oct 3, 1964.   R-28.
Religious and the Council; relationship to local
    bishop, America 106:66, Oct 21, 1961.   R-29.
Religious liberty, Cath Mind 62:2-3, Jan 1964.   R-30.
Religious liberty declaration, America 113:358-9,
    Oct 2, 1965.   R-31.
Religious life and renewal, New Blkfrs 47:2-4,
    Oct 1965.   R-32.
Reluctant revolutionary, Time 86:62-5, Sept 24,
    1965.   R-33.
The renewed liturgy, symposium, Hom Past Rev
    65:21-58, Oct 1964.   R-34.
Reply to R. A. Graham, Christian Cent 76:351,
    March 25, 1959.   R-35.
Reply to the Pope, Time 73:52, Feb 23, 1959.   R-36.
Reporting the Council, America 107:768, Sept 22,
    1962.   R-37.
R. S. V. P., Time 80:52, July 20, 1962.   R-38.

Response from the East, Tablet 213:162-63,
    Feb 14, 1959.   R-39.

Responsibility for the realization of local autonomy
    lies with the locals, not with the Romans, New
    Blkfrs 48:450-2, June 1967.   R-40.

Reunion in Rome, Newsweek 59:37, Jan 8, 1962.   R-41.

Revelation commission named; with list of new
    members of other commissions, Cath Mssngr
    81:1, Dec 27, 1962.   R-42.

A revolutionary Council; possible invitations to
    non-Catholics, Commonweal 75:270, Dec 8, 1961. R-43.

Ricca, P., Some reflections on De oecumenismo,
    Ref & Presb Wrld 28:305-14, Sept 1965.   R-44.

Richard, L., A sign among nations; schema on
    the Church, Spiritual Life 9:132-6, Summer 1963. R-45.

Richards, H., Vatican II and the Jews, Clergy
    Rev 49:552-61, Sept 1964.   R-46.

Richards, M., The Bishops of England and Wales
    and Christian unity, Clergy Rev 50:544-50,
    July 1965.   R-47.

Richardson, H., The Mother of the Church, Theol
    Dgst 14:60, Spring 1966.   R-48.

Richardson, W.J., The missionary Church and the
    Catholic teacher, Cath Educ 36:60-2, Oct 1965. R-49.

Richardson, W.J., Vatican II and the apostolic
    mission of the Church, Cath Sch J 66:43-7,
    April 1966.   R-50.

Riga, P., Catholics and anti-Semitism, US Cath
    30:19-20, June 1964.   R-51.

Riga, P.J., The Church Made Relevant, 1967
    Fides, $5.95.   R-52.

Riga, P.J., Church Renewed, 1967 Sheed, $5.50. R-53.

The right attitude to the Council, Tablet
219:1455-6, Dec 25, 1965.   R-54.

Right to worship according to one's conscience,
Time 84:90, Oct 2, 1964.   R-55.

Rijk, C., Catholics and Jews after 1967: a new
situation, New Blkfrs 50:15-26, Oct 1968.   R-56.

Riley, P., Commission plans a timetable for
Council's debates, Cath Mssngr 82:1, April 23,
1964.   R-57.

Riley, P., Vatican report, Columbia, Jan-Apr 1966. R-58.

Riley, P., Vatican II diary, Hom Past Rev
63:841-50, July 1963; 963-72, Aug 1963;
1031-41, Sept 1963.   R-59.

Riley, P., When East meets West; bishops from
the Eastern Rites at the Council, Lamp 62:10-11,
Jan 1964.   R-60.

Riley, T., Religious liberty: new name, old
teaching, Hom Past Rev 66:375-9, Feb 1966.   R-61.

Ripley, F.J., The Apostolate of the Laity, 1967
Sands, pb 9s 6d.   R-62.

Ritter, J., Return to Rome, Ave 98:5-9, Sept 14,
1963.   R-63.

Riudor, I., Membership in the Church in Lumen
Gentium, Theol Dgst 15:12-16, Spring 1967.   R-64.

Road from Trent to Rome, N.Y. Times Mag
p. 24-5, Nov 1, 1964.   R-65.

Road to Rome: observers at the Council, Newsweek
60:46, July 23, 1962.   R-66.

Roberts, H., Vatican II ecumenical relations, Lond
Q & HR 192:220-6, July 1967.   R-67.

Roberts, T.D., Council for survival, Commonweal
70:415-17, Aug 14, 1959.   R-68.

150

Roberts, T., The war for peace at the Council,
  Critic 25:58-63, Oct-Nov 1966.   R-69.
Roche, D., Life of a Council Father; Bp E.
  Primeau, Sign 43:11, Dec 1963.   R-70.
Roddy, J., Catholic revolution: authority of the
  bishops and supremacy of the Pope, Look
  29:21-7, Feb 1965. Reply: America 112:213,
  Feb 13, 1965.   R-71.
Roddy, J., How the Jews changed Catholic thinking,
  Look 30:18-23, Jan 25, 1966.   R-72.
Rodopoulos, P., The Pope and the observers,
  Tablet 218:1151, Oct 10, 1964.   R-73.
Rogers, V.D., Impact of Vatican II on Protestantism,
  Vital Speeches 33:91-4, Nov 15, 1966.   R-74.
Roman Catholics: peace or progress, Economist,
  216:1080, Sept 18, 1965.   R-75.
Rome and religious liberty, Christianity Tdy
  9:27-8, Dec 18, 1964.   R-76.
Rome: great battle of ideas, Life 57:4, Oct 23,
  1964.   R-77.
Rome letter; the eve of the Council, Tablet
  216:902-03, Sept 29, 1962.   R-78.
Root, H., Observing Vatican II. New Blkfrs
  46:11-14, Oct 1964.   R-79.
Rossano, P., What the II Vatican Council has
  taught regarding non-Christians, Christ to the
  Wrld 12:428-36, # 5, 1967.   R-80.
Roumanian bishops for the Council, Tablet 218:982,
  August 29, 1964.   R-81.
Round three, New Statesm 68:384, Sept 18, 1964.   R-82.
Roquette, R., Fresh orientation in the Church,
  Cath Wrld 196:343-50, March 1963.   R-83.

Rouquette, R., Priest sees Council in peril from
    Curia, Cath Mssngr 81:8, Aug 8, 1963.   R-84.
Rules for the execution of the cedree Perfectae
    Caritatis of the Second Vatican Council, Furrow
    17:668-75, Oct 1966.   R-85.
Rumble, L., Church reform; kung, Hom Past Rev
    62:1037-49, Sept 1962.   R-86.
Russian Orthodox attitude, Blkfrs 41:177-78,
    May 1960.   R-87.
Ryan, C., The Second Vatican Council and religious
    freedom, Blkfrs 45:355-67, Sept 1964.   R-88.
Ryan, L., Vatican II and the priesthood of the
    laity, Irish Theol Q 32:93-115, April 1965.   R-89.
Ryan, M. P., A Church to die in or live in? Cath
    Wrld, 203:17-21, April 1966.   R-90.
Ryan, M., Good news, Cath Mssngr, Dec 3, 1964.   R-91.
Ryan, M., What do you expect from the Council?
    St Joseph Mag 65:21-2, April 1964.   R-92.
Ryan, S., Vatican II: re-discovery of the episcopate,
    Irish Theol Q 33:208-41, July 1966.   R-93.
Ryan, V., The Divine Office; commentary on
    chapter 4 of the Vatican Council III constitution
    on the liturgy Doctrine & Life 14:107-14, Feb
    1964.   R-94.
Ryan, V., The liturgical year; commentary on
    chapter 5 of Vatican Council II constitution on
    the liturgy, Doctrine & Life 14:115-23, Feb
    1964.   R-95.
Rynne, X., Fourth Session, 1966 Farrar, Straus,
    $5.50.   R-96.
Rynne, X., Letter from Vatican City, New Yorker
    42:140, Oct 22, 1966, 41:135-6, 34-6, Sept 11;

Dec 25, 1965; 39:179-86; 123-4; 144; 88;
40:166; Sept 28, 1963 - Jan 9, 1965. 38:95-6,
Oct 20; 34-6, Dec 29, 1962.   R-97.

Rynne, X., Letters from Vatican City, 1963
Farrar, Straus, $3.95.   R-98.

Rynne, X., Second Session, 1964 Farrar, Straus,
$4.95.   R-99.

Rynne, X., Third Session, 1965 Farrar, Straus,
$4.95.   R-100.

Rynne, X., Vatican Council II, 1968 Farrar,
Straus, $10.00.   R-101.

Sahachern, H., The pill, Ave 101:5-8, May 15,
1965.   S-1.

St. John, H., After the Council: what? Lamp 1962.   S-2.

St. John, H., Ecumenical survey, Blkfrs 41:128-32,
April 1960.   S-3.

St. John, H., Towards Christian unity, Tablet
218:1398-9, Dec 12, 1964.   S-4.

St. Pius IX? Time 80:51, Aug 31, 1962.   S-5.

Sarkissian, A., Interview with the Armenian
observer, Cath Wrld 197:258-63, July 1963.   S-6.

Sartory, T., The Council and ecumenical concern,
Cross Currents 12:397-406, Fall 1962.   S-7.

Sasse, H., After the Council, Reformed Theol
Rev 25:1-14, Jan 1968.   S-8.

Sasse, H., Ecumenical challenge of the second
Vatican Council, Luth Wrld 12 - 2:107-19, 1965.   S-9.

Sasse, H., Second Vatican Council, Christianity
Tdy 7:4-7, Oct 12, 1962; Reformed Theol Rev
20:33-41, 65-78, Jun-Oct 1961.   S-10.

153

Sasse, H. , Sources of revelation, Reformed Theol
Rev 22:1-13, Feb 1963.   S-11.

Scarisbrick, J. , Post-Vatican II Catholicism, Dublin
Rev 516:117-28, Summer 1968.   S-12.

Schalk, A. , At the Council with Bishop Wright,
U. S. Cath 30:6-14, Feb 1965.   S-13.

Schalk, A. , Beyond the Council, U. S. Cath
30:6-11, May 1964.   S-14.

Schalk, A. , Troubleshooter for the Vatican: Card
Koenig, U. S. Cath 30:6-11, May 1964.   S-15.

Scharper, P. , The Catholic press after the Council,
Cath Mind 64:14-24, Sept 1966.   S-16.

Scharper, P. , The Council and the laity, Cath Mind
60:28-32, Sept 1962.   S-17.

Scharper, P. , The Council successes in making the
Church what it should have been at the end of
the 19th century, and wasn't, Critic 26:14,
Oct 1967.   S-18.

Scharper, P. , Framework for the future, Today
18:3-6, Oct 1962.   S-19.

Scharper, P. , Renewal of the Church, Commonweal
76:276-8, June 8, 1962.   S-20.

Scharper, P. , Second Vatican Council, Christianity
and Crisis 22:161-8, Oct 1, 1962.   S-21.

The schema on bishops and the government of
dioceses, The Pope Speaks 9:309-12, 1964.   S-22.

The schema on ecumenism, The Pope Speaks
9:312-5, 1964.   S-23.

The schema on ecumenism, Unitas 16:226, Fall
1964.   S-24.

Schema on ecumenism wins approval, Unitas
15:303-4, Winter 1963.   S-25.

The schema on religious freedom, Ave 102:16,
   Oct 9, 1965.   S-26.

The schema on the Church, The Pope Speaks
   9:306-9, 1964.   S-27.

Schema 13 revised, Tablet 219:249, Feb 27, 1965.   S-28.

Schepers, B. , Constitution on the sacred liturgy,
   Cath Theol Soc of Am Proceedings 19:211-4,
   1964.   S-29.

Schepers, B. , The mystery of the ecumenical
   Council: preparatory phase, Cath Wrld 194:209-15,
   Jan 1962.   S-30.

Schepers, B. , The second Council of the Vatican,
   Torch 43:4-8, Jan 1960.   S-31.

Schillebeeckx, E. , Church and mankind's future on
   earth, Cath Wrld 200:218-23, Jan 1965.   S-32.

Schillebeeckx, E. , The Layman in the Church and
   Other Essays, 1963, Alba, $2.95.   S-33.

Schillebeeckx, E. , Misunderstandings at the Council,
   Theol Dgst 11:131-4, Fall 1963.   S-34.

Schillebeeckx, E. , Open doors, closed doors and
   Vatican II, Cath Mind 62:23-7, Feb 1964.   S-35.

Schillebeeckx, E. , The Real Achievement of Vatican
   II, 1967, Herder and Herder, $2.95.   S-36.

Schillebeeckx, E. , Some liberal and conservative
   attitudes facing the Council, Cath Mssngr 81:5,
   Sept 26, 1963.   S-37.

Schillebeeckx, E. , Vatican II, 1963, Gill, $1.25.   S-38.

Schlink, E. , After the Council, 1968, Fortress,
   $4.95.   S-39.

Schlink, E. , Protestant view of the Vatican Council
   scheme De Ecclesia, Dial 3:136-42, Spring 1964.   S-40.

Schmemann, A., Reply to Burghardt, Theol Ed
   3:298-307, Winter, 1967.   S-41.

Schmidt, H., Past and future of the constitution on
   the sacred liturgy, Lumen 20:424-34, Summer
   1965.   S-42.

Schmitt, F., Church music and the constitution on
   liturgy, Caecilia 91:3-4, Spring 1964.   S-43.

Schmitt, F., Exit: Gregorian chant, Caecilia
   91:136-9, Winter 1965.   S-44.

Schmitz, W., Breviary after Feb 16: changes due
   to liturgy constitution, Priest 20:344-5, April
   1964.   S-45.

Schmitz, W., Recitation of prime: may be omitted,
   Priest 20:446, May 1964.   S-46.

Schmitz, W., Sunday vespers, Emmanuel 70:418,
   Oct 1964.   S-47.

Schomer, H., No setback to ecumenism by the
   Council, Unitas 16:63-4, Spring 1964.   S-48.

Schools and Vatican II, America 112:97, Jan 23,
   1965.   S-49.

Schruers, P., Our Council, yours and mine:
   collective responsibility, Lumen 17:623-36,
   Dec 1962.   S-50.

Schuler, J., What's going on over there at the
   Council? Friar 23:48-52, Feb 1965.   S-51.

Schutz, R., and Thurian, M., Revelation: A
   Protestant View, 1967, Newman, $4.50.   S-52.

Schutz, R., A Taize view of the Council, Tablet
   217:236, March 2, 1963.   S-53.

Scott, H., Report from Rome, Friar 18:59-62,
   Dec 1962.   S-54.

Scott, H., Roman sidelights, Friar 19:38-41, Jan
   1963   S-55.

Scott, J., The years after yesterday, Furrow
    17:705-11, Nov 1966.   S-56.

Scripture and tradition, America 113:456, Oct 23,
    1965.   S-57.

Seasoltz, K., Elasticity in liturgy and law, Liturg
    Arts 33:124-7, Aug 1965.   S-58.

Second Council of the Vatican in session 1962-1965,
    Social Just 58:371, Jan 1966.   S-59.

The Second Plenary Session: the Church begins to
    ask some questions, Cath Mssngr 80:5, Feb 8,
    1962.   S-60.

Second session, Commonweal 79:383-4, Dec 27,
    1963.   S-61.

Second Vatican Council, Christian Century 79:1247-8,
    Oct 17, 1962.   S-62.

Second Vatican Council, Economist 205:41-2, Oct 6,
    1962.   S-63.

The second Vatican Council, Furrow 17:53-5, Jan
    1966.   S-64.

Second Vatican Council, Hibbert J. 61:62, Jan 1963. S-65.

Second Vatican Council, Studies 54:349-52, Winter
    1965.   S-66.

Second Vatican Council, Tablet 213:972, Nov 7,
    1959.   S-67.

The second Vatican Council and Christian unity,
    Eastern Churches Q 14:1-2, Spring 1961.   S-68.

Second Vatican Council and the age, Am Bene Rev
    12:147-89, June 1961.   S-69.

Secretariate upgraded, America 107:1020, Nov 10,
    1962.   S-70.

Secular press at the Council, America 107:71,
    April 21, 1962.   S-71.

Seiner, J., What will they do about Church music?
Am Eccl Rev 151:373-7, Dec 1964.   S-72.

Sencourt, R., End of the Vatican Council, Contemporary Rev 208:31-5, Jan 1966.   S-73.

Sencourt, R., Report from the Vatican, Contemporary Rev 205:67-70, Feb 1964.   S-74.

Sencourt, R., Second Vatican Council, Contemporary
Rev 202:57-60, Aug 1962.   S-75.

Sencourt, R., Third session, Contemporary Rev
205:634-6, Dec 1964.   S-76.

Sencourt, R., What next at the Vatican? Contemporary Rev 204:113-4, Sept 1963.   S-77.

Sennott, R., The decree on the ministry and life
of the priest, Hom Past Rev 66:380-4, Feb 1966.   S-78.

Separated brothers, New Republic 145:7-8, Nov 6,
1961.   S-79.

Seppelt, J., and Roche, J., Vatican Council in
miniature, Cath Sch J 65:52-3, Nov 1965.   S-80.

Serafian, M., Pilgrim, 1964, Farrar Straus, $4.50. S-81.

Session IV for Vatican II Ave 100:16, Nov 7, 1964. S-82.

Seumois, X., Liturgy and missions, Lumen
20:487-98, Sept 1965.   S-83.

The seventeen schemata on the Council's agenda:
second session, Tablet 217:719-20, June 29, 1963. S-84.

Seventy-eight countries represented, Tablet
216:995-6, Oct 20, 1962.   S-85.

Shaping of the Council: preparatory progress,
Tablet 216:373-4, April 21, 1962.   S-86.

Sharing in the Council, America 109:227, Sept 7,
1963.   S-87.

Sharing the Council, Ave 96:16, Sept 15, 1962.   S-88.

Shea, G., Mary in the documents of Vatican II,
Marian Studies 17:20-6, 1966.   S-89.

Shea, G., Mary, Mother of the Church, Our Lady
Dgst 20:12-20, May 1965.   S-90.

Shea, G., Pope Paul and the Mother of the Church,
Marian Studies 16:21-8, 1965.   S-91.

Sheed, F., Distinguish what is essential in the
Church's teachings, Cath Mssngr 82:15, Aug 20,
1964.   S-92.

Sheen, F., Going back into Council: desiderata concerning the missions, Worldmission 14:3-8,
Summer 1963.   S-93.

Sheen, F., Missionary reflections on the Council,
Worldmission 14:3-8, Spring 1963.   S-94.

Sheen, F., Morticians of a conciliar decree,
Worldmission 17:3-17, Spring 1966.   S-95.

Sheerin, J., Card Spellman condemns anti-Semitism,
Cath Wrld 199:268-71, Aug 1964.   S-96.

Sheerin, J., Change strikes Catholic University,
Cath Wrld 205:132-3, June 1967.   S-97.

Sheerin, J., Communications decree: why the
dissent? Cath Wrld 198:267-71, Feb 1964.   S-98.

Sheerin, J., The Council moves into the twentieth
century, Christ to the World 196:204-8, Jan 1963.   S-99.

Sheerin, J., Council, the Church and the human
person: end of session observations, Cath Wrld
202:199-203, Jan 1966.   S-100.

Sheerin, J., Council's religious liberty document,
Cath Wrld 199:140-3, June 1964.   S-101.

Sheerin, J., The declaration on the Jews, Cath
Wrld 202:134-7, Dec 1965; reply 258-9, Feb
1966.   S-102.

Sheerin, J., Evangelical simplicity at the Council,
Cath Wrld 200:137-41, Dec 1964.   S-103.

Sheerin, J., How ecumenical will the Council be?
Cath Wrld 188:445-8, March 1959.   S-104.

Sheerin, J., The laity lose their chains, Cath
Wrld 202:262-6, Feb 1966.   S-105.

Sheerin, J., New Catholic image: openness to
today's world, Cath Wrld 198:204-7, Jan 1964.   S-106.

Sheerin, J., New secular ecumenism, Cath Wrld
203:261-4, Aug 1966.   S-107.

Sheerin, J., Our 100th anniversary and the new
era of the Holy Spirit, Cath Wrld 201:11-14,
April 1965.   S-108.

Sheerin, J., Pope John opens the Council, Cath
Wrld 196:139-43, Dec 1962.   S-109.

Sheerin, J., Pope Paul: firm and realistic, Cath
Wrld 198:75-9, Nov 1963.   S-110.

Sheerin, J., Pope Paul's progressive speech opening
the third session, Cath Wrld 200:73-7, Nov 1964. S-111.

Sheerin, J., Protestant hopes for the fourth session,
Cath Wrld 202:5-9, Oct 1965.   S-112.

Sheerin, J., Protestant thinking on the eve of the
Council: the WCC Central Committee meeting,
Cath Wrld 196:3-6, Oct 1962.   S-113.

Sheerin, J., Protestants and the Council, Cath Wrld
195:196-9, July 1962.   S-114.

Sheerin, J., Religious liberty moves forward,
Cath Wrld 202:70-3, Nov 1965; reply 202:194,
Jan 1966.   S-115.

Sheerin, J., Shall we wrangle or reason about
reforms? Cath Wrld 199:203-6, July 1964.   S-116.

160

Sheerin, J., Through renewal to reunion, Cath
  Wrld 196:68-72, Nov 1962.   S-117.
Sheerin, J., The Vatican Council: a new Easter,
  Cath Mssngr 82:4, March 26, 1964.   S-118.
Sheerin, J., What happened to session three?
  Cath Wrld 200:200-4, Jan 1965.   S-119.
Sheerin, J., What has the Council accomplished?
  Cath Wrld 196:268-72, Feb 1963.   S-120.
Sheerin, J., What's next for the Council? Cath
  Layman 77:14-21, Sept 1963.   S-121.
Sheerin, J., Will the bishops speed up renewal?
  Cath Wrld 204:132-3, Dec 1966.   S-122.
Shehan, L., Pastoral on Christian unity, Cath
  Mssngr 80:4, Jan 11, 1962.   S-123.
Shephard, L., The new look in liturgy, Tablet
  217:1349-50, Dec 14, 1963; replies March 7;
  March 21, 1964.   S-124.
Shepherds and fishermen: conflicts of emphasis
  in St Peter's, Tablet 216:1179-80, Dec 8, 1962.   S-125.
Sheridan, T.L., On understanding the Council:
  Danielou's address on the decree on the Church,
  America 112:122, Jan 23, 1965.   S-126.
Sheridan, W., The decree on mission activity,
  Irish Eccl Rev 106:109-25, Aug 1966.   S-127.
Sherman, F., Church in the modern world, Dialog
  5:195-200, Spring 1966.   S-128.
Sherry, R., Active participation of the faithful in
  Mass, Priest 20:959-61, Nov 1964.   S-129.
Sherwood, P., Church in Council: Vatican II, En-
  counter 24:441-57, Autumn 1963.   S-130.
Shinn, R., Hopes for the second Vatican Council,
  Christianity and Crisis 22:157-9, Oct 1, 1962.   S-131.

Shortening the Council, Tablet 218:372-3,
     April 1964.   S-132.

Should the Jews be grateful to Catholics? Rabbi
     Denburg says no, Ave 99:5, April 4, 1964.   S-133.

Significant correction: norms to regulate interim
     work, America 108:358-9, March 16, 1963.   S-134.

Sillem, A., The practice of ecumenism, Clergy
     Rev 52:193-5, March 1967.   S-135.

Simon, M., Vatican Council II: Eppur si muove,
     Modern Churchman 8:190-6, April 1965.   S-136.

Sims, B., Birth and rebirth, Jubilee 14:28-31,
     Nov 1966.   S-137.

Simultaneous translation in St. Peter's, Tablet
     217:1160, Oct 26, 1963.   S-138.

Siri, G., Truth first and always, America
     108:434-5, March 30, 1963.   S-139.

Sixth session ends: Central Preparatory Commis-
     sion, Tablet 216:507, May 26, 1962.   S-140.

Skima, A., The Greek observer on the Council,
     Tablet 218:1122, Oct 3, 1964.   S-141.

Skinner, J., The Church in dialogue, Month 31:48-9,
     Jan 1964.   S-142.

Skydsgaard, K., Address, Unitas 15:218-20, Fall
     1963.   S-143.

Skydsgaard, K., Last intention of the Council, J
     Ecumenical Studies 3:151-4, Winter 1966.   S-144.

Skydsgaard, K., Mystery of the Church, J Ecumenical
     Studies 1:405-23, Autumn 1964.   S-145.

Skydsgaard, K., Neglected dimensions in De Ecclesia,
     J Ecumenical Studies 1:111-2, Winter 1964.   S-146.

Skydsgaard, K., The Papal Council and the Gospel,
     1961, Augsburg, $3.95.   S-147.

Slow, D. , Roman Diary, America 116:582-3,
   April 22, 1967; 117:18-19, July 1.   S-148.

Sloyan, G. , The constitution on the sacred liturgy
   and prayer-life in college, Soc Cath College
   Teachers of Sacred Doctrine Proceedings 107-121,
   1964.   S-149.

Sloyan, G. , The Magna Charta of the liturgy,
   Guide 192:8-11, Nov 1964.   S-150.

Sloyan, G. , The Secular Priest in the New Church,
   1967, Herder and Herder, $5.95   S-151.

Sloyan, G. , Worship in a New Key, 1967, Herder
   and Herder, $3.95; Image $.95.   S-152.

Smedt, E. , Ecumenical dialogue, Cath Mind
   61:55-8, April 1963.   S-153.

Smedt, E. , The emerging Church: interview with
   the Bishop of Bruges, Tablet 221:522-4, May 13,
   1967.   S-154.

Smet, W. , The Council and unity, Lumen 17:637-42,
   Dec 1962.   S-155.

Smith, E. , Vatican II speaks for all Christians,
   J Ecumenical Studies 2:470-1, Fall 1965.   S-156.

Smith, F. , Vatican II: introduction, Thomist
   27:vii-xiii, April 1963.   S-157.

Smith, H. , The ascent to God after the Council,
   America 116:283-5, Feb 25, 1967.   S-158.

Smith, K. , Dominican prelates and experts at the
   Council, Torch 47:4-7, Jan 1963.   S-159.

Smith, T. , Let's take the cursing out of the liturgy,
   Nat Cath Reporter 3:6, Feb 1, 1967.   S-160.

Smith, V. , The woman and the Council: will her
   voice be heard? Ave 100:26-30, Oct 3, 1964.   S-161.

Snell, A., The liturgical constitution and sacred
music, Liturgy 33:64-7, July 1964.   S-162.

The Spanish bishops and religious liberty, Tablet
218:1420, Dec 12, 1964.   S-163.

A special section on the second Vatican Council,
Sign 44:10-35, Sept 1964.   S-164.

Speeding the Council, America 109:2, July 6, 1963.   S-165.

Speed-up: third session, Time 84:70, Sept 18, 1964.   S-166.

Spina, T., The Pope and the Council, 1963, Barnes,
$12.50.   S-167.

Spiritual bouquet for the Ecumenical Council,
Columbia 42:7, Dec 1962.   S-168.

Spiritual growth through the Council's liturgical
renewal, Sacred Heart Messenger 99:10-12,
Dec 1964.   S-169.

Stack, J., Implications of the present ecumenical
mood for religious education, Hartford Q 6:20-9,
Summer 1966.   S-170.

Stanley, D., Authority in the Church: a New
Testament reality, Cath Biblical Q 29:555-73,
Oct 1967.   S-171.

Statement on anti-Semitism ready for Council
fathers, Cath Mssngr 81:8, Oct 24, 1963.   S-172.

The states of perfection, education and ecumenism
report of the seventh session of the Central Preparatory Commission, Cath Mssngr 80:5, Sept 6,
1962.   S-173.

Steere, D., A Quaker looks at the Vatican Council,
Religion in Life 33:569-76, Autumn 1964.   S-174.

Stefun, B., Previews of the Council, Cath Ed
33:160-1, Oct 1962.   S-175.

Stein, W., The Council and the bomb, New Blkfrs

47:68-83, Nov 1965.   S-176.

Stein, W., Would you press the button? Worldview
7:4-15, Dec 1964.   S-177.

Steiner, W., German opinion: Wort und Wahrheit
survey, Blkfrs 43:289-92, June 1962.   S-178.

Stockwood, A., Half-time at the Vatican, Contemporary Rev 203:230-2, May 1963.   S-179.

Stransky, T., and Nelson, C., Catholic-Protestant
conversation America 106:186-9, Nov 11, 1961;
235, Nov 18.   S-180.

Stransky, T., The Council's time of decision, Sign
44:14-7, Sept 1964.   S-181.

Stransky, T., A critical turn in Vatican II, Sign
43:16-23, Oct 1963.   S-182.

Stransky, T., Declaration on Religious Freedom,
1967, Paulist, $.95.   S-183.

Stransky, T., The decree on ecumenism: an
analysis, One in Christ 1:5-26, 1966.   S-184.

Stransky, T., The decree on ecumenism, Clergy
Rev 51:3-26, Jan 1966.   S-185.

Stransky, T., Promoting Christian unity: the work
of the Secretariate, America 104:733-4, March 4,
1961.   S-186.

Stransky, T., Session 4: the pace quickens, Sign
44:19-23, Sept 1965.   S-187.

Stransky, T., Third session: time for decisions,
Doctrine and Life 14:409-20, Sept 1964.   S-188.

Stransky, T., Vatican Council 1962: preparation
phase, Wiseman 236:203-16, Fall 1962.   S-189.

Stransky, T., What they said about the Council,
Cath Layman 77:10-19, April 1963.   S-190.

Stransky, T., The wonderful communion of the
faithful, Cath Wrld 202:48-51, Oct 1965.   S-191.

Streamling St. Peter's: effects of the first session,
Tablet 217:1056-7, Oct 5, 1963.   S-192.

Stroup, R., Reply to Card Bea, Christian Century
79:1487-8, Dec 5, 1962.   S-193.

Stroynowski, J., The Catholic Church and the modern
world, New Times 11-13, March 15, 1967.   S-194.

Stroynowski, J., The Vatican and the modern world,
New Times 9-11, Jan 19, 1966.   S-195.

Stuber, S., The Council one year later, Commonweal
85:368-72, Jan 6, 1967.   S-196.

Stuber, S., Vatican dialogue, Christian Century
81:1405, Nov 11, 1964.   S-197.

Student ecumenical Council research committees,
Shield 43:8, suppl, Dec 1963.   S-198.

Subilia, V., Ecclesiology of Vatican II, Reformed
and Presbyterian Wrld 28:200-10, March 1965.   S-199.

Subilia, V., New Catholic synthesis and the function
of Protestantism, Reformed and Presbyterian
Wrld 29:6-12, March 1966.   S-200.

Subilia, V., Problem of Catholicism, 1964, West-
minster, $4.50.   S-201.

Subsidiarity at the Council: Card Koenig on centralization, America 104:686, Feb 25, 1961.   S-202.

Success of the Council: Holy Father's prayer in-
tentions: see issues of Sacred Heart Messngr
beginning Jan 1962.   S-203.

Suddenly a chill, Ave 100:16-7, Sept 26, 1964.   S-204.

Suenens, L., Co-responsibility in the Church, 1968,
Herder and Herder, $4.95.   S-205.

Suenens, L., The Council and Church unity,
Criterion 3:3-11, Spring 1964.   S-206.

Suenens, L., The Council and Church unity, Dublin
Rev 239:144-61, Summer 1965.   S-207.

Suenens, L., The Council and pastoral renewal,
New City 3:4-9, May 1, 1964.   S-208.

Suenens, L., Council to speak out on war and peace,
Cath Mssngr 81:1, May 23, 1963.   S-209.

Suenens, L., Holy Spirit's role, Cath Mssngr 82:1,
May 7, 1964.   S-210.

Suenens, L., Interview, U.S. Cath 31:16-18,
March 1966.   S-211.

Suggestions for change by the clergy of Freiburg,
Perspectives 6:22-3, Dec 1961.   S-212.

Sullivan, J., Vatican II: the setting, View 26:14-5,
Sept 1962.   S-213.

Sullivan, K., The Constitution and religious life,
Nat Liturg Week 25:252-7, 1964.   S-214.

Sullivan, O., Behind the Council: secrecy-shrouded
preparations, Jubilee 10:6-8, Oct 1962.   S-215.

Summary report of sixth session of the Central
Preparatory Commission, Cath Mssngr 80:1,
May 17, 1962.   S-216.

Summons from Rome, Time 78:47, Dec 29, 1961.   S-217.

Supreme realist, Time 80:40, July 6, 1962.   S-218.

Sweeney, O., Structure of the Church: pastoral
reflection, Christus Rex, 19:285-8, Oct 1965.   S-219.

Syrian Orthodox against De Judaeis, Tablet
218:1184, Oct 17, 1964.   S-220.

Taking the Council's moving picture, Christian
Century 81:1229, Oct 7, 1964.   T-1.

Tanenbaum, M. , Discussion of Judaism in the
Council, Shield 44:38, Oct 1964.   T-2.

Tanebaum, M. , A rabbi looks at the Council,
Lamp 61:10-11, Jan 1963.   T-3.

Tansy, A. , Voice of the Council: apostolate of the
tertiary, Fran Herald and Forum 42:202-6, July
1963.   T-4.

Tapia, R. , Burning issues of Schema 13, Hom
Past Rev 66:739-53, June 1966.   T-5.

Tapia, R. , Theology of Vatican II, Hom Past Rev
67:207-12, Dec 1966.   T-6.

Tarte, R. , Postconciliar Priest, 1966, Kenedy,
$3. 95.   T-7.

Tavard, G. , Commentary on De Revelatione, J
Ecumenical Studies 3:1-35, Winter 1966.   T-8.

Tavard, G. , Church Tomorrow, 1967, Herder and
Herder, $3. 95; Doubleday-Image $. 85.   T-9.

Tavard, G. , Council's declaration on non-Christians,
J Ecumenical Studies 3:160-6, Winter 1966.   T-10.

Tavard, G. , Ecumenical meeting may mark beginning
of a new era, Jubilee 6:8-15, April 1959.   T-11.

Tavard, G. , Evolution in moral theology, Cath Wrld
203:29-32, April 1966.   T-12.

Tavard, G. , The mystery of the Church in the
liturgical constitution, Worship 39:11-6, Jan 1965. T-13.

Tavard, G. , Our Lady, Cath Mssngr 82:1, Oct 1,
1964.   T-14.

Tavard, G. , Pilgrim Church, 1967, Herder and
Herder, $4. 95   T-15.

Tavard, G. , Scripture and tradition in pastoral

168

perspective, Cath Wrld 198:14-20, Oct 1963. T-16.

Tavard, G., Vatican II: the end of the Counter-
Reformation, Cath Mssngr 80:5-6, Nov 15, 1962. T-17.

Tempest stirred by Council statement on the Jews
in Syria, Cath Mssngr 83:2, Dec 24, 1964. T-18.

Tennant, E., Can the press serve the Council?
Cath Wrld 197:107-13, May 1963. T-19.

Test of good-will: proposed declaration on anti-
Semitism, Time 84:63, Oct 9, 1964. T-20.

Texas Bp Levin blasts unity critics, Cath Mssngr
82:7, Dec 5, 1963. T-21.

Themes in ecclesiology and liturgy from Vatican II,
Worship 41:66-84, Feb 1967. T-22.

Theological implications of the experience of the
first session, Eastern Churches Q 14:382-3,
Winter 1962. T-23.

Theory and practice: l'Osservatore Romano and
Lombardi's suggestion for the Council, Commonweal 75:480, Feb 2, 1962. T-24.

These latest Council decrees, America 113:518-9,
Nov 6, 1965. T-25.

Third and last session? America 110:476-7,
April 4, 1964. T-26.

Third session of the Central Commission, Tablet
216:91, Jan 27, 1962. T-27.

Thirteen still unlucky, Tablet 219:1082-3, Oct 2,
1965. T-28.

Thirty votes on collegiality, Tablet 218:1122-3,
Oct 3, 1964. T-29.

Thomas, J., What did the Council say on contraception? America 114:294-6, Feb 26, 1966. T-30.

Thomas, J., Vatican II and ecumenism, Reformed
and Presbyterian Wrld 28:210-14, March 1965.　T-31.

Thomas, R., The Council, 20th century renaissance,
Lamp 61:8-9, Jan 1963.　T-32.

Thompson, A., and DeRoche, E., Education of
Sisters and Vatican II, Cath Educ Rev 66:96-100,
Feb 1968.　T-33.

Thompson, B., Many questions about the ecumenical
Council, Nat Council Outlook 9:23-4, March 1959.　T-34.

Thompson, B., Vatican Council and the separated
brethren, Drew Gateway 37, 1-2:1-19, 1966-7.　T-35.

Thorman, D., The Council and the family,
Marriage 44:26-31, Sept 1962.　T-36.

Thorman, D., Today's layman: an uncertain Catholic,
America 116:39-41, Jan 14, 1967.　T-37.

Thorman, D., What lay people want in the Church,
Sign 41:11-13, Oct 1961.　T-38.

Thornhill, J., The mystery of Mary and the Church,
Hom Past Rev 67:31-40, Oct 1966.　T-39.

Thorny path to Church unity, Christianity and Crisis
20:14-6, Feb 22, 1960.　T-40.

Thoughts by a Russian theologian: Schmemann,
America 101:629, Aug 22, 1959.　T-41.

Three Anglican churchmen picked as Council observers, Cath Mssngr 80:1, July 12, 1962.　T-42.

3 cardinals get liturgy positions, Cath Mssngr 82:1,
Feb 6, 1964.　T-43.

Three German bishops signed anti-schema leaflet
on communications media, Tablet 217:1139,
Dec 7, 1963.　T-44.

Three views of Vatican II, Christianity Tdy
12:28-9, June 7, 1968.　T-45.

Through a glass darkly: Soviet Literary Gazette
replies to critics, Tablet 217:43-4, Jan 12, 1963. T-46.

Thurian, M., Ecumenism and the Council, Month
31:171-6, March 1964. T-47.

Thurian, M., Vatican II and ecumenical dialogue,
Way 20:24-9, April 1964. T-48.

Tierney, M., The Council and the Mass, 1967,
Dimension, $3.00. T-49.

Tillard, J., A point of departure, Rev Religion
26:424-40, May 1967. T-50.

Time essay, How Vatican II turned the Church
toward the world, Time 86:24-5, Dec 17, 1965. T-51.

A Time for reflection: putting the Council into
effect in Germany, Tablet 220:1465-7, Dec 31,
1966; reply 221:79-80, Jan 21, 1967. T-52.

Time table at St. Peter's: approaching the
scriptural questions, Tablet 216:1097-8,
Nov 17, 1962. T-53.

Time to be counted, America 110:178-9, Feb 8,
1964. T-54.

To be continued, Newsweek 64:91, Nov 2, 1964. T-55.

To the Council fathers: Pope Paul VI's discourse
opening the second session, America 109:412,
Oct 12, 1963. T-56.

To warm hearts, Newsweek 53:82, Feb 9, 1959. T-57.

Toland, T., The second Vatican Council and
seminary liturgical life, Nat Liturg Week
24:208-13, 1963. T-58.

Tompkins, J., Sacred music and the constitution,
Worship 38:289-96, April 1964. T-59.

Too much with us? schema on the Church and the
world, Tablet 218:1253-4, Nov 7, 1964. T-60.

Topics for the Council: 2nd and 3rd sessions of
the Preparatory Commission, Clergy Monthly
26:94-100, April 1962.   T-61.

Topics for the Council: the 4th and 5th sessions
of the Central Commission, Clergy Monthly
26:166-71, June 1962.   T-62.

Topics for the Council: the 6th session of the
Preparatory Commission, Clergy Monthly
26:256-60, August 1962.   T-63.

Topics for the Council: the 7th session of the
Preparatory Commission, Clergy Monthly
26:292-6, Sept 1962.   T-64.

Toward a responsible laity, Commonweal 81:403-4,
Dec 18, 1964.   T-65.

Toward dialogue, America 111:766, Dec 12, 1964.   T-66.

Toward reform, Newsweek 62:101, Oct 21, 1963.   T-67.

Toward the second Vatican Council, Ecumenical
Rev 14:429-79, July 1962.   T-68.

Towards the third session, Tablet 218:260-1,
March 7, 1964.   T-69.

Tracy, R., American Bishop at the Vatican Council,
1967, McGraw, $6.50.   T-70.

Tracy, R., Council debate on the Church in the
modern world, America 113:461, Oct 23, 1965.   T-71.

Tracy, R., The Council on Christian education,
America 113:432-3, Oct 16, 1965.   T-72.

Tracy, R., The debate on religious liberty,
America 113:397-9, Oct 9, 1965.   T-73.

Tracy, R., Early report from Rome and the
Council, America 113:330, Sept 25, 1965.   T-74.

Tracy, R., Failure of session three, America
112:284-6, Feb 27, 1965.   T-75.

Tracy, R., Has the Council lost its steam?
America 110:162-4, Feb 1, 1964.   T-76.

Tracy, R., Letter from the Council, America
113:364; 397-9; 432-3; 566-7; 706; 774-5;
Oct-Dec 1965.   T-77.

Tracy, R., Naturalism and schema 13, America
113:432, Oct 16, 1965.   T-78.

Tracy, R., The nature of peace and schema 13,
America 113:706, Dec 4, 1965.   T-79.

Tracy, R., Postscript on the Council, America
114:40, Jan 8, 1966.   T-80.

Tracy, R., The schema on religious liberty,
America 113:364, Oct 2, 1965.   T-81.

Tracy, R., Vatican City: progress report, America
113:461, Oct 23, 1965.   T-82.

Tradition reprieved, Tablet 218:1132-3, Oct 10,
1964.   T-83.

Trafford, D., The lay apostolate, Tablet 220:64-5,
Jan 15, 1966.   T-84.

The training of priests, Tablet 218:1075-6,
Sept 26, 1964.   T-85.

Traveller's joy: schema on the Church in the
modern world, Tablet 218:1192-3, Oct 24, 1964.   T-86.

Treinen, S., Underestimate a woman: the Council
didn't, Priest 22:797-9, Oct 1966.   T-87.

Trend against juridical powers for bishops' conferences, Cath Mssngr 82:6, Nov 21, 1963.   T-88.

Trend towards factual analysis in Vatican II,
Herder 4:45-7, Feb 1967.   T-89.

Tucci, R., Political and civil aspects of the
Church in renewal, Cath Wrld 207:61-4,
April 1968.   T-90.

Tucek, J. , Bible interpretation poses problem for
the Council, Cath Mssngr 81:7, Oct 2, 1963.   T-91.

Tucek, J. , Blueprint of Council mailed, Cath
Mssngr 80:1, July 19, 1962.   T-92.

Tucek, J. , Curia criticized, Cath Mssngr 81:6,
Nov 14, 1963.   T-93.

Tucek, J. , Eastern Rites a big question, Cath
Mssngr 81:12, Sept 19, 1963.   T-94.

Tucek, J. , Mission bishops seek understanding,
Cath Mssngr 81:12, Sept 26, 1963.   T-95.

Tucek, J. , The New Pentecost, St. Jude 28:7-11,
Oct 1962.   T-96.

Tucek, J. , Pope reorganizes Council commissions
discussion on ecumenism, Cath Mssngr 82:4,
Nov 28, 1963.   T-97.

Turn of the Roman tide, Economist 209:1007-8,
Dec 7, 1963.   T-98.

Turner, D. , The Church in the World, 1968,
Scepter, 25s.   T-99.

Turnstile, M. , Vatican news gathering, New
Statesman 70:514, Oct 8, 1965.   T-100.

21st century, Time 73:54-5, Feb 9, 1959.   T-101.

Two Armenian observers, Tablet 217:1075,
Oct 5, 1963.   T-102.

Two Jewish leaders voice concern, Cath Mssngr
82:8, June 4, 1964.   T-103.

Two new members, Tablet 216:1059, Nov 3, 1962.   T-104.

Two new postconciliar bodies, Tablet 221:51-2,
Jan 14, 1967.   T-105.

Unequivocal statement needed on religious
  freedom: German moral theologians, Tablet
  218:480, April 25, 1964.   U-1.
Unfinished business, America 112:159, Jan 30, 1965. U-2.
Unfinished Council business, Christian Century
  81:1389-90, Nov 11, 1964.   U-3.
Unfinished reformation, Time 83:66, Feb 7, 1964.   U-4.
Unforeseeable decade since Pius XII, America
  119:310, Oct 12, 1968.   U-5.
Unger, D., The concept of the priesthood: changed
  by Vatican II? Hom Past Rev 67:497-502,
  March 1967.   U-6.
Unger, D., The constitution on the sacred liturgy,
  Priest 21:35-40, Jan 1967.   U-7.
U.S. journalists criticize schema on communica-
  tions media, Tablet 217:1302-3, Nov 30, 1963.   U-8.
Unity reaches mid-century plateau, Christian
  Century 80:36, Jan 9, 1963.   U-9.
Unity under-secretariates for Orthodox and
  Protestants, Tablet 217:378-9, April 6, 1963.   U-10.
Unity, unison and the Council: comparison with
  1870, Tablet 215:223-4, March 11, 1961.   U-11.
Unprecedented changes, America 108:323, March 9,
  1963.   U-12.
Updating the Church, America 107:259, May 19,
  1962.   U-13.
Uses of ambiguity: revelation and religious liberty,
  Time 86:78, Nov 5, 1965.   U-14.

Vagaggini, C., The Council and liturgy reforms, Cath Mssngr 81:5, Dec 20, 1962. V-1.

Vagaggini, C., General principles for liturgical reform, Furrow 14:79-88, Feb 1963. V-2.

Vajta, V., Interpretation of the Vatican Council, Luth Wrld 13-4:412-30, 1966. V-3.

Valabek, R., An on-the-scene report, Scapular 23:29-32, Jan 1964. V-4.

Vanbergen, R., Conciliar constitution on the liturgy and the liturgical movement in other Churches, One in Christ 1:367-89, 1965. V-5.

Vanbergen, R., Constitution on the liturgy and the Faith and Order reports, Studia Liturg 5:1-19, Spring 1966. V-6.

Van Dusen, H., Visit to Vatican II, Christianity and Crisis, 23:230-1, Dec 9, 1963. V-7.

Van Weers, A., Karl Barth goes to Rome, Frontier 10:91-5, Summer 1967. V-8.

Vassady, B., God, Church and world: clues for conversation and cooperation, Theol and Life 9:10-25, Spring 1966. V-9.

The Vatican Council: a new age for lay Catholics, Sign 42:11-39, Oct 1962. V-10.

Vatican Council adopts decree on communication, Publishers' Weekly 185:60-1, Jan 6, 1964. V-11.

Vatican Council and the press, Tablet 216:164, Feb 17, 1962. V-12.

Vatican Council is of and for the Roman Catholic Church, Christian Century 79:513, April 25, 1962. V-13.

Vatican Council: liberal or conservative? Dominicana 48:171-2, Fall 1963. V-14.

Vatican Council: no disaster, Economist
213:950, Nov 28, 1964.   V-15.

Vatican Council: no more crusades, Economist
217:363-4, Oct 23, 1965.   V-16.

Vatican Council progresses, Christian Century
81:1293, Oct 21, 1964.   V-17.

Vatican Council: the perplexed Pope, Economist
215:746, May 15, 1965.   V-18.

Vatican Council to be covered by John Cogley,
Editor and Publisher 97:34, Sept 5, 1964.   V-19.

Vatican Council: what it means, U. S. News
53:68-71, Oct 22, 1962.   V-20.

Vatican Council's field of vision, Christian Century
81:1197, Sept 30, 1964.   V-21.

Vatican Council's start, Economist 205:1007-8,
Dec 8, 1962.   V-22.

Vatican Council II makes progress, Christian
Century 80:1325, Oct 30, 1963.   V-23.

Vatican ecumenical Council concludes first session,
Unitas 14:299-301, Winter 1962.   V-24.

Vatican officials act to keep Orthodox informed,
Cath Mssngr 81:1, Jan 17, 1963.   V-25.

Vatican II, Dialog 5:169-216, Summer 1966.   V-26.

Vatican II: a hard look at the Church, Sign 43:10,
Oct 1963.   V-27.

Vatican II and missions, America 111:444-5,
Oct 17, 1964.   V-28.

Vatican II and the bomb, Month 34:271-3, Nov 1965. V-29.

Vatican II and the laity, America 103:367, June 18,
1960.   V-30.

Vatican II and U. S. peace aims, America 113:701
Dec 4, 1965.   V-31.

Vatican II: first session, America 107:1240-1,
Dec 15, 1962.   V-32.

Vatican II: legacy of John XXIII, Senior Scholastic
83:3, Nov 1, 1963.   V-33.

Vatican II: Oct 11, 1962, America 106:637,
Feb 17, 1962.   V-34.

Vatican II: part III, Commonweal 81:3-4, Sept 25,
1964.   V-35.

Vatican II progress note, Hom Past Rev 62:251,
Dec 1961.   V-36.

Vatican II: stage 4: a symposium, Sign 45:10-37,
Sept 1965.   V-37.

Vatican II: summation, Ave 102:16-7, Sept 11, 1965.   V-38.

Vatican II: the final stretch, America 113:486,
Oct 30, 1965.   V-39.

Vatican II warms up, Christian Century 79:1472,
Dec 5, 1962.   V-40.

Vatican II's test, Newsweek 66:55-6, Sept 20, 1965.   V-41.

Vaticanum II: formal convocation, America 106:429,
Jan 6, 1962.   V-42.

Vatican III? theologians congress to determine
meaning of Council documents, Newsweek 68:104,
Oct 10, 1966.   V-43.

Vatican with emphasis on Council secrecy, Christian
Century 79:1122, Sept 19, 1962.   V-44.

Vatican without walls, Christian Century 80:3-4,
Jan 2, 1963.   V-45.

Vatican's dilemma, Christian Century 82:859-60,
July 7, 1965.   V-46.

Vatican's riches, Economist 216:168, July 10, 1965.   V-47.

Vedernikov's analysis in the Journal of the Moscow
Patriarchate, Tablet 217:690, June 22, 1963.   V-48.

Velde, P., The lay deacon, Jubilee 11:22-3,
April 1964.   V-49.

Verdict on the fathers, Economist 217:1057-8,
Dec 4, 1965.   V-50.

Verghese, P., Aggiornamento and the unity of all,
Ecumenical Rev 15:377-84, July 1963.   V-51.

Vermilye, T., Pray brethren, Altar and Home
27:27-32, Jan 1960.   V-52.

Vernacular at Mass, America 106:392-3, Dec 16,
1962.   V-53.

Vexation stronger than persecution, Tablet 218:1185,
Oct 17, 1964.   V-54.

Villain, M., De Oecumenismo at the second session,
Eastern Churches Q 16:191-201, 1964.   V-55.

Vischer, L., Address of the WCC representative,
Unitas 14:296-8, Winter 1962.   V-56.

Vischer, L., After the fourth session, Ecumenical
Rev 18:150-89, April 1966.   V-57.

Vischer, L., Ecumenical frontiers, America
109:277, Sept 21, 1963.   V-58.

Vischer, L., Report on second Vatican Council,
Ecumenical Rev 16:43-59, Oct 1963.   V-59.

Vischer, L., World Council of Churches and the
Vatican Council, Ecumenical Rev 14:28-95,
April 1962.   V-60.

Vogel, A., Second Vatican Council on the nature
of the Church and ecumenism, Anglican Theol
Rev 49:243-62, July 1967.   V-61.

Vokes, F., An Anglican view, Irish Theol Q
32:156-61, April 1965.   V-62.

Vokes, F., A separated brother and the Council,
Doctrine and Life 14:294-303, May 1964.   V-63.

Von Allmen, J., The dogmatic constitution Lumen
Gentium, J Ecumenical Studies 4:650-83, Fall
1967.   V-64.

Von Feldt, E., The press and the second session
of Vatican II, Cath Press Assn 5:6-7, 1964.   V-65.

Vorgrimler, H., Commentary on the Documents of
Vatican II, 5 vols, 1968- Herder and Herder,
$39.95.   V-66.

Vote against prejudice, Time 86:61, Oct 22, 1965.   V-67.

Voting on De Ecclesia, Tablet 218:1151, Oct 10,
1964.   V-68.

Voting on De Oecumenismo, Tablet 218:1152, Oct 10,
1964.   V-69.

Vox populi: vox Dei! America 106:35, Oct 14, 1961.   V-70.

Vuccino, A., Church unity, Cath Mind 61:59-61,
April 1963.   V-71.

Waal, V., De Ecclesia: an Anglican comment,
One in Christ, 1:31-43, 1966.   W-1.

Wagner, J., The Church and the Liturgy, 1967,
Paulist, $4.50.   W-2.

Wagner, J., The Council speaks, Cath Educ
36:6-7, Dec 1965.   W-3.

Wagner, J., Vatican II and the schools, Cath
Educ 35:151, Oct 1964.   W-4.

Wagner, J., Vatican II debate, Cath Educ 35:398-9,
Jan 1965.   W-5.

Walgrave, V., Dominican Self-Appraisal in the
Light of the Council, 1968, Priory, $10.00.   W-6.

Wall, A., Aggiornamento in the chancery, America
118:637, May 11, 1968.   W-7.

Wall, B., and Lucas, B., Thaw at the Vatican,
    1964, Verry, $6.00.   W-8.

Walsh, D., Reply to O'Hanlon, America 109:441,
    Oct 9, 1963.   W-9.

Walsh, L., Sacraments and sacramentals, Doctrine
    and Life 14:95-107, Feb 1964.   W-10.

Walsh, L., Willing observance of Council's decrees,
    Sacred Heart Mssngr   98:10-12, Nov 1963.   W-11.

Warlock, D., The post-conciliar priest, Dublin
    Rev 516:129-40, Summer 1968.   W-12.

Wary rapport, Newsweek 60:68-9, Dec 3, 1962.   W-13.

Waugh, E., Same again please, National Rev
    13:429-32; 521; 14:37, Dec 1962, Jan 1963;
    Commonweal 77:487-9, Feb 1, 1963; America
    108:440, March 30, 1963.   W-14.

Weakland, R., Music and the constitution, Nat
    Liturg Week 25:204-9, 1964.   W-15.

Weakland, R., Music and the constitution on the
    liturgy, Liturg Art 33:7-9, Nov 1964.   W-16.

Weakland, R., Situation, attitudes and hurdles,
    Sacred Music 93:53-8, Summer 1966.   W-17.

Weber, T., Questions for Vatican II, Worldview
    7:4-15, Dec 1964.   W-18.

Wedge, F., The family and the ecumenical Council,
    Fam Dgst 18:32-6, Oct 1962.   W-19.

Weeks of decision: voting statistics, Tablet
    218:1300-1, Nov 14, 1964.   W-20.

Weigel, G., Church power comes from the Spirit,
    Cath Mssngr 81:9, Nov 21, 1963.   W-21.

Weigel, G., The Council on anti-Semitism, America
    109:70-1, July 20, 1963.   W-22.

Weigel, G. , How is the Council going? America
109:730-2, Dec 7, 1963.   W-23.

Weigel, G. , Nature of the Church to be clarified,
Cath Mssngr 81:9, Sept 26, 1963.   W-24.

Weiser, F. , The Council and the liturgy, Tdy Fam
39:17-21, Dec 1964.   W-25.

Weiss-Rosmarin, T. , Ecumenism and the Jews,
Ramparts 3:58-64, Summer 1964.   W-26.

Wenger, A. , Second Vatican Council, 1966, Newman,
$5. 50.   W-27.

Werwage, W. , The liturgy: summit and source of
Christian life, Nat Liturg Week 25:260-2, 1964.   W-28.

Wesselmann, R. , Changes in the Sunday sermon,
Pastoral Life 12:52-4, Nov 1964.   W-29.

Whalen, J. , The press opens up Vatican II,
Journalism Q 44:53-61, Spring 1967.   W-30.

Whalen, W. , Second Vatican Council: round-up
report, Information 76:14-21, Sept 1962.   W-31.

What about the concordats? Christian Century
82:1244, Oct 13, 1965.   W-32.

What Africa expects from the Council, Tablet
216:822, Sept 1, 1962.   W-33.

What the American bishops are saying, Cath Mssngr
81:5, Dec 27, 1962.   W-34.

What Belgians ask of the Council, Cath Mssngr 80:3,
Oct 18, 1962.   W-35.

What Canadians ask of the Council, Cath Mssngr
80:17, Nov 22, 1962.   W-36.

What did the Council say about the missions?
Shield 45:6-8, April 1966.   W-37.

What Germans ask of the Council, Cath Mssngr
80:7, Oct 11, 1962.   W-38.

What Ireland expects of the Council, Cath Mssngr
    80:3, Oct 25, 1962.   W-39.

What is a bishop? Christian Century 79:1024,
    Aug 29, 1962.   W-40.

What next for the layman? Cath Layman 80:19-20,
    June 1966.   W-41.

What price Council? beatification of Pius IX,
    Christian Century 79:1087-8, Sept 12, 1962.   W-42.

What the Council cost, Tablet 219:1428-9, Dec 18,
    1965.   W-43.

What the Council did, Newsweek 66:60, Dec 20,
    1965.   W-44.

What the Council did not discuss, Tablet 219:1429,
    Dec 18, 1965.   W-45.

What the new Council decree means and its urgency,
    Lamp 62: 16-7, Feb 1964.   W-46.

What the Portuguese, expect, Cath Mssngr 80:9,
    Nov 8, 1962.   W-47.

What went wrong? Time 82:52, Dec 6, 1963.   W-48.

Wheeler, G. , Token for good, Tablet 216:954-4,
    Oct 13, 1962.   W-49.

Whelan, M. , Index of Scripture texts in Vatican II
    documents, Bible Tdy 28:1975-90, Feb 1967.   W-50.

When East meets West, Tablet 218:668, June 13,
    1964.   W-51.

When the Council reconvenes will a new Church
    be born? Newsweek 60:54-6, Dec 17, 1962.   W-52.

While the cable editor slept, America 113:67,
    July 17, 1965.   W-53.

White House to Vatican, America 107:870, Oct 13,
    1962.   W-54.

White, P., The Council and marriage,
Marriage 44:54-6, August 1962.   W-55.

White, P., Thoughts about the Council, Jubilee
9:2-4, March 1962.   W-56.

Why collegiality is so important, Sign 44:35-6,
Jan 1965.   W-57.

Why not open-end Vatican II? Christian Century
81:132, Jan 29, 1964.   W-58.

Wiebler, W., Spreading the fire, Today 18:10-12,
Oct 1962.   W-59.

Williams, A., Reply to Polish, Christian Century
83:84-5, Jan 19, 1966.   W-60.

Williams, G., An Anglican looks at the ecumenical
Council, Ave 95:5-8, March 31, 1962.   W-61.

Williams, G., Time to rend and time to sew, Cath
Mssngr 81:5-6, March 7, 1963.   W-62.

Wills, G., Journalists report the Council, Nat
Rev 15:572-4, Dec 31, 1963; correction 16:124,
Feb 11, 1964.   W-63.

Wiltgen, R., The case for Pope Paul, St. Anthony
74:50-7, Feb 1967.   W-64.

Wiltgen, R., The Divine Word News Service, Cath
Press Assn 5:10-11, 1964.   W-65.

Wiltgen, R., The press and the general public are
hungry for information, Christ to the World
8:205-17, 1963.   W-66.

Wiltgen, R., The Rhine Flows into the Tiber, 1966,
Hawthorn, $6.95.   W-67.

Winkley, A., Directions in Church building since
the Vatican Council, Dublin Rev 516:141-54,
Summer 1968.   W-68.

Winter, J. , The Council and the priest,
Perspectives 9:52-5, March 1964.   W-69.

The witness to revelation, Tablet 218:991-2,
Sept 5, 1964.   W-70.

Wojnar, M. , Decree on the Oriental Churches,
Jurist 25:173-255, April 1965.   W-71.

Wolleh, L. , and Schmitz, E. , Council: A Documentation in Pictures and Text of the Second
Vatican Council, 1966, Viking, $38.50.   W-72.

Women in the Church, America 107:972-3, Nov 3,
1962.   W-73.

Woodruff, D. , A cloud at the close, Tablet
218:1337-8, Nov 28, 1964.   W-74.

Woodruff, D. , The Council accepts the closure,
Tablet 217:1112-3, Oct 19, 1963.   W-75.

Woodruff, D. , The Council and the rights of con-
sciences, Tablet 218:1104-5, Oct 3, 1964.   W-76.

Woodruff, D. , The Council takes its time, Tablet
216:1036-7, Nov 3, 1962.   W-77.

Woodruff, D. , Council's second month, Tablet
216:1069-71, Nov 10, 1962.   W-78.

Woodruff, D. , Cross-currents in the Council,
Tablet 218:1309-10, Nov 21, 1964.   W-79.

Woodruff, D. , The day of the periti, Tablet
219:1318-9, Nov 27, 1965; replies 1423, Dec 18;
1451, Dec 25; 220, Jan 1, 1966.   W-80.

Woodruff, D. , Declaration on religious freedom,
Tablet 220:121-3, Jan 29, 1966.   W-81.

Woodruff, D. , Episcopal self-confidence, Tablet
217:1196-7, Nov 9, 1963.   W-82.

Woodruff, D. , The episcopate looks at itself,
Tablet 217:1085-6, Oct 12, 1963.   W-83.

Woodruff, D. , The fathers disperse and reflect
on whence they came, Tablet 219:1376-8,
Dec 11, 1965.   W-84.

Woodruff, D. , First days of the Council, Tablet
216:980-2, Oct 20, 1962.   W-85.

Woodruff, D. , No national blocks in the Council,
Tablet 216:1008-10, Oct 27, 1962.   W-86.

Woodruff, D. , Second Vatican Council: at the third
session, Intr Affairs 41:223-35, April 1965.   W-87.

Woodruff, D. , The third session: a changed and
more tranquil mood, Tablet 218:1076-8, Sept 26,
1964.   W-88.

Woodruff, D. , Troubling the waters: Council debates
the laity, Tablet 217:1140-2, Oct 26, 1963.   W-89.

Word to outsiders, Time 82:64, Nov 22, 1963.   W-90.

Worden, T. , Revelation and Vatican II, Scripture
19:54-62, April 1967.   W-91.

Work, M. , Lay apostolate is Council topic, Cath
Mssngr 80:8, Nov 8, 1962.   W-92.

Works of the Liturgical Commission, Worship
36:356-8, April 1962.   W-93.

The world and the Council: meeting new needs,
America 107:920, Oct 20, 1962.   W-94.

World Council Central Committee welcomes the
Vatican Council and Unity Secretariate, Unitas
12:204-7, Fall 1960.   W-95.

WCC meeting told unity hopes somewhat lessened
by encyclical, Cath Mssngr 82:6, Sept 3, 1964.   W-96.

The world, Europe, Rome: the Council and non-
essentials, Tablet 216:27-8, Jan 13, 1962.   W-97.

World poverty and the Christian, Commonweal
81:215, Nov 13, 1964.   W-98.

World poverty and Vatican II, Cath Charities
    Rev 48:2-3, Oct 1964.   W-99.

Worlock, D. , Aggiornamento in embryo, Wiseman
    Rev 237:316-34, Winter 1963.   W-99a.

Worlock, D. , English Bishops at the Council, 1965,
    Burns, 10s 6d.   W-100.

Worlock, D. , The priest, Dublin Rev 516:129-40,
    Summer 1968.   W-101.

Worlock, D. , The Vatican Constitution on the Church
    and the layman in the Church, Clergy Rev 50:836-43,
    Nov 1965.   W-102.

Wright, J. , Conciliar Rome, America 112:418-25,
    March 27, 1965.   W-103.

Wright, J. , Seed time and Spring time, Tablet
    220:411-3, April 9, 1966.   W-104.

Wright, J. , Student editors quiz Bp Wright, Cath
    Educ 36:21-3, May 1966.   W-105.

Wright, J. , Vatican Council, Look 26:55-6,
    Oct 23, 1962.   W-106.

Wright, J. , Vatican II and youth, Cath Educ
    34:263-5, Nov 1963.   W-107.

Wright, J. , Vatican II in 24 seed ideas, Hom
    Past Rev 67:23-30, Oct 1966.   W-108.

Wright, L. , New Churches for old: architectural
    implications of the liturgy decree, Tablet 218:180-1,
    Feb 15, 1964; replies 248-9, Feb 29; 304,
    March 14; 332, March 21.   W-109.

Wright, M. , The Church Today, 1967, Lawrence,
    $1.34.   W-110.

Yes, we do expect a lot from the Council,
Ave 99:17, April 18, 1964.   Y-1.

Young, G. , Liturgy; an achievement, America
110:14-15, Jan 4, 1964.   Y-2.

Young, G. , Two bishops speak, America 110:14-16,
Jan 4, 1964.   Y-3.

Your private devotions, America 111:686, Nov 28,
1964.   Y-4.

Yzermans, V. , American contributions to the
decree on the ministry and life of priests, Am
Eccl Rev 155:145-63.   Y-5.

Yzermans, V. , American Participation in the Second
Vatican Council 1967, Sheed and Ward $16. 50.   Y-6.

Yzermans, V. , Americans at the third session,
Extensn 59:40-3, Jan 1965.   Y-7.

Yzermans, V. , Bishops at Vatican II, Hom Past
Rev 63:490-7, March 1963.   Y-8.

Yzermans, V. , Bringing the Council to mainstreet,
Extensn 60:10-12, Dec 1965.   Y-9.

Yzermans, V. , Christmas at the Council: Council
message is renewal, reunion, reality, Columbia
44:8, Dec 1964.   Y-10.

Yzermans, V. , Council accomplishments, Mission
Dgst 31:2-7, Feb 1963.   Y-11.

Yzermans, V. , Council conversation: Diekmann,
Kung, Murray and Weigel, Ave 100:10-11, Oct 3,
1964.   Y-12.

Yzermans, V. , The eve of the Council, Today's
Family 37:2-7, Oct 1962.   Y-13.

Yzermans, V. , A layman reflects on the Council:
John Cogley, Columbia 44:14, Sept 1964.   Y-14.

Yzermans, V., New force in the Church: missionary bishops at the Council, Today's Family 38:14-19, Jan 1963. Y-15.

Yzermans, V., A New Pentecost 1963, Newman $6.50. Y-16.

Yzermans, V., The observers: friendly guests, keen critics, Sign 43:24-31, Oct 1963. (Reply by H. Scott Charles, Jan 1964). Y-17.

Yzermans, V., A parish priest reports to his people on Vatican II, Duke Div Rev 29:20-6, Winter 1964. Y-18.

Yzermans, V., Patron saints: Gregory Nazianzen, John Chrysostom, Gregory the Great, Crosier 36:16-22, March 1961. Y-19.

Yzermans, V., Pope John's Council; the four opening addresses, Am Bene Rev 13:550-57, Dec 1962. Y-20.

Yzermans, V., The Pope's invitation to church unity; the coming Council, Hom Past Rev 61:1149-52, Spring 1961. Y-21.

Yzermans, V., The press and Vatican II, Cath Press Assn 4:4-7, 1963. Y-22.

Yzermans, V., Vatican II: where now? Columbia 46:14-16, Jan 1966. Y-23.

Yzermans, V., A visit to the Vatican Council 1963, Catechetical Guild, $.50. Y-24.

Zahn, G., Davy Crockett and the bishop, Ramparts 3:62-5, March 1965. Z-1.

Zavitz, L., Emphasis was on diversity, Christianity Tdy 8:30-2, Dec 6, 1963. Z-2.

Zavitz, L., Vatican view of authority, Christianity Tdy 8:36-7, Nov 22, 1963. Z-3.

Zeitlin, S., Ecumenical Council Vatican II and
the Jews, Jewish Q Rev 56:93-111, Oct 1965.   Z-4.

Zerr, B., Second Vatican Council, St. Joseph
62:9-11, August 1961.   Z-5.

Zimmermann, G., American princes of the Church,
Look 29:24-8, August 24, 1965.   Z-6.

Zogby, E., Vatican II, the anawin and Christian
holiness, Chicago Studies 6:87-97, Spring 1967.   Z-7.

Zuroweste, A., Fact and fancy about the Vatican
Council, Social Just 57:51-2, May 1964.   Z-8.

Subject Index

Africa, A-37, C-44, H-134, M-205, N-80, P-4, W-33, Y-14.

Agenda, A-23, B-192, P-121, S-60, S-117, T-92.

Alfrink, Card., A-32-35, P-3.

altar, M-113.

Anabaptists, F-81.

Anglican, A-38, A-56, A-57-8, E-47, G-58, K-16, M-120,
    M-179, P-25-27, P-107, T-42, V-61-63, W-1, W-16.

Announcement of Council, A-16, E-5, J-22, L-71, P-64-66,
    P-72, P-75, R-36, T-34, T-57, T-101.

anti-Semitism, see: Jews.

Arabs, A-68-70, D-27, J-10, J-59, P-124.

architecture, C-27, C-102, M-18, M-50, N-21, R-34,
    W-68, W-109.

Armenia, S-6, T-102.

art, B-12, C-27, C-176, F-60, F-67, H-59, L-16,
    M-63-64, M-72, O-96, R-6, R-34.

Asia, C-97, C-314, D-60, D-81, D-104, D-116, I-7,
    L-102, M-205, P-11, S-6, Y-14.

atheism, A-74, H-56, H-58.

Australia, P-47.

Austria, A-6, A-83, K-49.

authority, B-29, B-128, B-217, C-299, D-37, E-1, E-46,
    H-22, K-9, K-12, M-228, O-31, R-22, R-71, S-171,
    S-202, Z-3.

Baptism, B-133-134.

Baptist, J-1, S-164.

191

Barth, K. , B-13-16, V-8.

Basque, A-63.

Baum, G. , B-21-56, S-164.

Bea, Card. B-57-72, B-133-134, B-153, C-31-37, C-145,
O-60, P-3, P-136, R-14, S-193.

Belgium, B-81, S-154, W-35.

Bible, A-40, B-129, B-222, C-101, C-307, D-100, E-3,
F-6, F-10, H-128, H-136, L-82, M-55, M-234, O-39,
O-41, O-95, P-96, S-57, S-147, S-171, T-16, T-91,
W-50, see also: revelation; tradition.

biography, A-12, B-199, B-205, C-253, D-20, D-112,
E-14, F-68, L-37, O-8, P-3, R-70, S-13, V-10, W-100,
Z-6.

birth control, B-21, B-101, C-105, F-58, H-23, H-85,
L-88, M-9, M-41, N-49, S-1, T-30, see also: marriage.

bishops, A-11, B-23, B-46, B-89, B-105, B-107, B-121,
B-150, B-185, B-217, C-119, C-140, F-74, H-40, H-44,
J-27, K-34, K-77, L-3, L-20, L-92, M-176, O-31,
O-68, O-80, P-9, P-62, P-85, R-29, R-40, R-71, R-93,
S-22, S-122, T-88, T-92-93, W-7, W-40, W-82-83,
Y-8.

books evaluated, B-136, B-229, C-14, C-18, C-52, C-66,
C-185, C-237, D-16, D-82a, D-131, E-11, G-26, G-57,
L-41, L-58, M-1, P-130, P-140.

breviary, A-4, B-167, C-53, C-102, C-176, R-34, R-94,
S-45-47.

Buddhists, O-104.

Calvin, John, M-20.

Canada, B-108, C-5, C-24, D-1, L-1, L-62, L-65, N-47,
O-61, O-74, W-36.

canon law, A-1, M-32, M-52, O-85-86, P-33, P-78.

Cardijn, Card. , B-81.

catechetics, A-85, C-65-66, C-102, D-10, J-44, L-68,
 L-83, M-119, M-168, M-196, P-116.

Catholic Press Association, P-142.

celibacy, C-89, see also: priests.

censorship, F-3, N-69, see also: religious freedom.

Central Preparatory Commission, A-84, B-107, C-77,
 C-90-95, C-112, C-203, C-318, E-43, J-40-41, P-38,
 P-76, P-104, R-19, S-140, S-173, S-216, T-27, T-61-
 64.

chancery, W-7.

charity, H-36.

China, A-14, C-235.

Christian unity, see: ecumenism.

church and state, M-229, see also: politics; religious
 freedom.

Church, Dogmatic Constitution, A-30, A-41, A-75, B-30,
 B-156, B-219, B-226, C-6, C-11, C-152, C-168, C-180,
 C-199, C-259, D-8, D-17, D-32, D-51, D-100, E-41,
 E-50, F-27, F-48, G-2, G-22, G-62, H-92, H-97, K-35,
 K-77, L-57, M-3, M-29-30, M-57, M-60-61, M-213,
 M-223, M-234, R-45, R-50, R-64, S-27, S-40, S-108,
 S-126, S-145-146, T-15, V-61, V-64, V-68, W-1, W-24,
 W-102.

Church, modern, A-59, B-44, B-140, B-160, B-170,
 C-100, C-104, C-114, C-138, C-147, C-311, D-7, D-14,
 D-31, D-36, D-45, D-79, D-110, E-45, F-14, F-53-54,
 F-83, G-24, G-56, H-39, H-62, H-84, H-87, H-137,
 J-18, J-62, K-6, K-52, K-77, L-58, L-94, M-6, M-76,
 M-89, M-117, M-132, M-134, M-166, M-228, N-10,
 N-24, N-79, O-10, O-54, S-28, S-99, S-106, S-128,
 S-194-195, S-219, T-5, T-28, T-51, T-60, T-71, T-78,

T-86, T-99, U-13, V-9, V-27, W-52, W-94.

clericalism, P-133.

closing of the Council, B-31, P-14, P-18, P-22, P-83,
S-73, W-84, see also: Vatican II, 4th sess.

collegiality, B-3, B-23, B-30, B-40, B-89, B-109, B-138,
C-130, C-153, D-30, D-51, D-94, D-129, E-28, F-8,
F-16, G-50, H-55, K-34-35, M-28, M-108, Q-3, S-205,
T-29, W-57, W-82, see also: bishops.

commissions, A-42, C-148, C-224, F-16, H-121, I-12,
J-24, J-36, L-70, M-6, M-106, P-63, R-42, S-70,
T-97, T-105, W-93.

common good, M-39.

communications, see: press.

Communism, A-53, C-150, C-225, D-74, J-57.

concelebration, B-77, B-106.

Confraternity of Christian Doctrine, C-157.

Congar, Yves, C-158-164, J-61.

conscience, see: religious freedom.

conservative, B-6, B-141, B-161, C-126, C-300, D-58,
D-130, E-38, E-56, K-59-60, M-24, N-43, P-81, P-91,
R-11, S-34, S-37, S-125, V-14, W-14.

contemplative life, P-34.

converts, B-163, C-87, O-7.

convocation of the Council, J-25, N-9, O-51, P-70, V-34,
V-42, W-85, see also: Vatican II, 1st sess.

Coptic Church, C-186, D-27

Cordeiro, Abp., A-8.

Council of Christians and Jews, H-65.

critics of the Council, A-39, A-62, B-99, B-102, B-125-
127, B-154, B-178, B-190, B-202, B-220, C-67, C-69,
C-87, C-265-266, D-15, D-22, D-113, E-48, F-69,
G-21, G-38, G-57, H-119, K-74, L-44, L-90, M-23,

194

D-41, D-59, D-82, D-124, D-127, E-12, E-21, F-30,
F-39, F-61, G-34, G-49, H-14, H-15a, H-33, H-45,
H-52, H-104, H-110, H-122, H-143-144, I-6, I-11, J-2,
J-46, K-4, K-8, K-41, K-67, K-70, L-32, L-34, L-40,
L-46, L-63, L-85, M-15, M-19, M-34, M-38, M-47,
M-59, M-137, M-144, M-153, M-167, M-194, M-199,
N-1, N-36, N-39, N-75-77, O-5, O-30, O-33, O-69-70,
P-88, R-44, R-67, S-4, S-7, S-23-25, S-48, S-79,
S-107, S-123, S-135, S-155, S-170, S-184-186, S-191,
S-206-207, T-21, T-31, T-35, T-40, T-47, U-9, V-51,
V-55, V-58, V-61, V-63, V-69, V-71, W-19, W-26,
W-49, W-51, Y-10, Y-21.

education, A-25, A-85, B-74, B-175, B-203, B-209, C-166,
C-182, C-200, C-234, D-3-4, D-42, D-49, D-70, D-97-
99, D-108, E-37, G-8, G-16, H-141-142, H-145, J-65,
K-27, L-68, L-83, L-95, M-116, M-118, M-148, P-6,
P-45, R-49, S-49, S-80, S-97, S-149, S-170, S-173,
S-198, T-33, T-72, W-4, W-59, W-107.

efficiency, E-22.

elections, O-31.

England, B-171, C-32, C-87, I-9, R-47, W-100.

episcopacy, see: bishops.

episcopal conferences, F-74-75.

Episcopalian, see: Anglican.

eschatology, M-234.

Eucharist, B-212, B-215, C-176-177, C-228, D-66, G-12,
G-63, H-3, M-21, M-113, R-34, S-129, T-49, V-53.

Europe, C-75, C-96, F-40, W-97.

experts, B-102, B-142, C-230, E-57, F-28, J-58, P-77,
S-159, W-80.

faith, C-59, H-78, O-19.

family, see: marriage.

Finland, L-62, L-65.

France, B-117, C-42, F-80, F-90.

freedom, see: religious freedom.

Germany, B-79, C-197, G-17-18, M-206, S-178, S-212,
    T-44, T-52, U-1, W-38, W-56.

Gibbon, Edward, H-41.

Greek Orthodox, A-36, G-6, G-53-55, I-1, J-66, M-190,
    N-23, S-141, see also: Orthodox.

Gregorian chant, S-44, see also: music.

Haring, Bernard, H-22-27, H-132, M-163.

Heenan, Card., E-45, H-64-73.

historical perspective, A-36, B-20, C-173, C-193, C-330,
    F-38, H-21, H-76, H-95, H-97, K-40, L-14, M-78,
    M-195, M-212, Q-1, S-18, S-59, S-164, W-72.

Holland, see: Netherlands.

Holy Spirit, C-26, G-5, L-42, M-101, M-220, P-35, S-108,
    S-210, T-96, W-21, Y-16.

human dignity, A-60, B-207, C-46, H-113, M-227, S-100,
    see also: religious freedom.

humility, B-162.

Hungary, H-133.

implementation, see: results of Council.

Index, The, F-3.

inter-communion, B-25, E-17, L-43, O-72.

Ireland, C-116, C-292, L-57, W-39.

iron curtain countries, A-14, B-111-112, C-232, C-335,
    I-16, J-57, M-187, R-81.

Israel, D-27, F-33, I-20-22, L-29, see also: Jews.

197

C-44, C-80, C-131, C-135, C-315, D-43, D-90, F-50,
F-52, G-22, G-43-44, G-69, H-19, H-46, H-103, I-5,
J-45, K-13, K-21, K-45, L-4-5, L-20, L-24-27, L-35,
L-84, M-16, M-25, M-147, N-34, N-54, N-59, O-46,
O-61, O-72, Q-4, R-62, R-89, S-17, S-33, S-105,
S-129, T-4, T-37-38, T-65, T-84, V-10, V-30, V-70,
W-41, W-89, W-92, W-102, Y-14.

Latin, K-48, L-9, N-46, S-138.

Latin America, B-135, M-31, R-21.

legalism, H-132, O-85.

Leger, Card., C-40, D-1, L-36-37, V-10.

liberal, B-6, C-126, C-136, F-13, K-60, K-77, L-51,
N-67, P-81, P-91, P-123, S-35, V-14.

Lichtenberger, Bp., B-56.

Lienart, Card., A-13, D-48, L-56.

Lindbeck, G., E-44, L-59-67.

liturgical year, H-112, R-34, R-95.

liturgy, A-1, A-37, A-64, B-9, B-33, B-131, B-143,
B-159, C-91, C-102, C-165, C-170, C-176-177, C-188,
C-202, C-204, C-272, C-293-298, C-313, D-55, D-65-67,
D-87, D-89, D-126, E-54, F-32, F-76, F-87, G-2,
G-12, G-58, G-63, G-73, H-7, H-9, H-53, H-112,
H-123, L-22-23, L-42, L-64, L-74-81, L-89, M-19,
M-42-51, M-65, M-67, M-70, M-80, M-86, M-91,
M-94-97, M-113, M-151, M-200, M-202, M-216, O-22-
24, P-21, P-49, P-116, P-130, R-7, R-25, R-34, S-29,
S-42, S-58, S-124, S-129, S-149-150, S-152, S-160,
S-169, T-13, T-22, T-43, U-7, V-1-2, V-5-6, W-2,
W-25, W-28, W-93, Y-2.

Lombardi, R., K-62, T-24.

Lutheran, D-120, E-8, F-59, H-98, J-52, L-33, L-65,
L-98-100, M-82, Q-2, S-9, S-143, V-3.

McIntyre, Card. , E-18.

magisterium, P-68.

marriage, B-2, B-107, C-105, D-46, D-92, F-2, F-84, G-60,
H-23, H-42, I-2, M-35, M-41, M-100, M-162, T-36,
W-55.

Mary, B. V. , A-45, A-72, B-5, B-34, C-58-63, C-144,
C-285-286, C-289, F-9, F-42-43, H-77, H-129, I-19,
K-11, K-51, K-54, L-17, L-19, M-38, M-114-115, P-37,
P-54, P-141, R-48, S-89-91, T-14, T-39.

Mass, see: concelebration; Eucharist; liturgy; missal; music.

medicine, F-22, H-16.

Melkites, O-8.

Methodist, H-90, N-15, O-104.

missal, B-167.

missions, A-22, A-31, B-11, B-45, B-76, C-91, C-212-213,
C-246, D-68, D-81, E-9, E-27-33, F-47, G-11, G-35,
G-51, G-66, H-47, H-99-102, H-107, J-41, K-7, K-19,
L-8, L-47, M-62, M-159-160, M-205, N-20, N-51, P-46,
P-88, R-49-50, S-83, S-93-95, S-127, T-95, V-28, W-37,
W-79, Y-15.

Mohammedans, B-17.

morals, J-49, O-10, R-28, T-12.

music, A-46, B-86, C-102, C-176, K-26, M-68-69, M-73,
O-50, O-109, P-56, P-122, R-34, S-43-44, S-72, S-162,
T-59, W-15-17.

Mystical Body, C-35.

Nestorians, N-16.

Netherlands, B-113-116, E-13.

Newman, Car. , B-90, B-128, K-20.

non-Christian religions, D-6, D-64, D-128, E-34, G-62,
H-69, M-167, M-180-181, N-48, O-35, P-11, R-27, R-80,
T-10.

obedience, C-38.

observers, A-36, A-49, A-56-58, B-43, B-91, B-133,
   B-148, B-184, C-332, D-53, F-70, F-90, G-27, G-40, G-69,
   J-11, J-66, K-39, L-69, M-183, M-189, N-50, N-54,
   N-57, O-1, O-12-18, O-91, O-105, P-26, P-71, P-128,
   R-66, R-73, R-79, S-6, S-144, S-190, T-102, V-56,
   W-62, Y-17.

Orthodox, A-36, A-54, B-100, D-72, G-13-15, H-28, I-23,
   L-43, L-85, M-87, M-129, M-141, N-37-40, N-44, O-17,
   O-72, O-87-92, P-72, P-105, R-87, S-220, U-10, V-25,
   V-51, see also: Eastern Churches. Greek Orthodox.

Ottaviani, Card., C-41, E-56, F-18, L-73, O-98-99.

papacy, B-89, B-174, K-1, L-92, M-110, M-141, M-182,
   O-2, P-82, R-71, S-167.

parish, B-173, C-102, C-113, C-142, C-177, C-268, C-315,
   D-73, D-88-89, G-75, H-30, J-26, J-45, K-46, L-7,
   L-50, L-78, L-80, M-152, M-198, O-38, R-34, S-208,
   S-219, T-16.

Paschal Mystery, H-112.

pastoral, see: parish.

Paul VI, Pope, B-78, C-123, C-136, F-91, G-59, H-40,
   H-116, M-173-174, M-164, N-19, N-27, N-71, P-12-24,
   P-69, P-81-85, S-91, S-110-111, S-203, T-56, W-64.

Paulists, S-108.

Peace, B-45, B-139, C-109, E-35, F-31, G-42, H-61,
   J-29, J-37, M-140, O-11, O-66, R-69, R-75, S-176,
   S-209, T-79, V-31.

perfection (Christian), C-8, C-223, G-73, H-26, J-20, J-30,
   M-55, M-149, M-170, S-158, S-169, S-173, Z-7.

Philippines, A-15, C-3, F-87.

Pius IX, Pope, W-42.

Pius, XII, Pope, U-5.

pluralism, J-18, L-87.

Poland, P-57, P-59-60.

politics, C-205, L-45, M-109, M-215, M-229, N-68, P-93,
S-34, T-90, W-32.

population, C-106, M-184, P-86.

Portugal, W-47.

post-conciliar, see: results of Council.

poverty, A-26, A-73, C-317, G-16, N-56, O-56, R-21,
V-47, W-98-99.

prayer, B-56, C-116, C-325, E-47, P-94-95, R-17, S-149,
S-203, W-11, Y-4.

preaching, L-77, L-80, P-96, W-29.

preparation for the Council, A-17-18, A-23, A-61, A-84,
B-26, B-84, B-147, B-172, C-4, C-19, C-22, C-72, C-84,
C-93, C-113, C-146, C-181, C-243, C-274, C-288,
C-313, D-5, D-54, D-61, D-117, E-5, F-1, F-7, F-19,
F-45, F-51, G-45-46, H-13, H-20, J-28, J-32, K-25,
K-56, K-65, L-49, L-67, L-96, M-8, M-142, M-155,
M-173, M-214, N-8, N-42, N-66, O-20, P-97-106,
P-121, R-43, R-68, S-3, S-10, S-30, S-69, S-86, S-104,
S-175, S-189, S-213, S-215, T-11, T-68, V-13, V-36,
V-52, Y-13, see also: Central Preparatory Comm.

Presbyterian, N-30, P-44, P-108, R-24, S-200.

press, A-65, B-8, B-32-33, B-186, C-78, C-81, C-91,
C-123, C-143, C-149, C-214-216, C-269, C-275, C-282,
C-287, C-308, C-318, D-2, D-21, F-15, F-17, F-25,
F-66, H-83, H-118, J-39, J-41, J-43, K-3, K-18, K-55,
K-57, L-6, L-38-39, L-90, M-36, M-46, M-81, M-121-
122, M-154, M-165, M-169, M-172, M-203, M-217, N-3,
N-28-29, N-72, P-77, P-109-114, P-129, P-142, R-15,
R-18, R-37, S-16, S-71, S-98, T-1, T-19, T-44, T-100,

U-8, V-11-12, V-19, V-44, V-65, W-30, W-65-66, W-105, Y-22.

priestly formation, see: seminaries.

priests, A-3, A-8, B-19, B-45, B-217, C-88-89, C-241, D-101, G-23, H-67, H-140, K-77, L-50, L-77, L-80, M-152, M-210, N-53, P-5, P-31, P-133, S-78, S-151, S-212, T-7, U-6, W-29, W-69, W-101, Y-5.

Protestants, B-61, B-63, B-67, B-87, B-96, B-123-124, B-149, B-180, B-187, B-202, C-1, C-63, C-314, C-324, C-329, C-334, D-121, G-11, G-18, H-97, H-109, I-24, K-29, L-69, M-112, M-133, M-135-136, M-146, M-197, N-7, N-12, N-47, N-57, O-101, P-7, P-72, P-125-128, Q-1, R-74, S-8, S-40, S-53, S-112-114, S-131, S-136, S-180, S-200, U-10, V-5, V-45-46, V-59, W-8, W-58, see also: denominational names.

prudence, F-21.

psychiatry, C-88, C-320-321.

Quakers, S-174.

race, C-99, C-115, C-208, D-85, G-41, H-139, I-14, M-124, M-140, O-3, R-1, V-67.

Rahner, Karl, R-2-3, S-14.

reform, A-37, B-188, B-199, C-311, D-83, D-86, D-122, E-23, E-44, F-74, I-5, J-54, J-60, K-70, L-64, L-66, M-3, M-43, M-48, M-80, M-94, M-97, M-126, N-69, O-6, O-64, O-93, O-106, R-12, R-20, R-65, S-116, T-17, T-67, U-4.

religious freedom. B-83, B-94, B-128, B-189, B-208, C-25, C-46, C-50, C-54-57, C-107, C-139, C-167, C-171, C-201, C-301, C-303, C-328, D-35, D-52, D-95, D-106, F-56, F-78-79, F-86, H-64, H-73, H-89, H-95, H-108,

H-130, H-146, J-4, J-29, K-17, K-24, K-33, K-43,
L-52, L-72, L-87, M-14, M-54, M-85, M-99, M-150,
M-224, M-226-233, N-69, P-115, R-29, R-30-31, R-55,
R-61, R-76, R-88, S-26, S-101, S-115, S-163, S-183,
T-73, T-81, U-1, W-32, W-74, W-76, W-81.

religious life, A-81, B-98, B-129, C-49, C-70, C-125,
C-172, C-222, D-12, D-126, F-44, G-3, H-63, H-92,
H-123, J-30, K-30, L-10, M-138, M-186, O-25, O-83-
84, P-33, P-34, R-32, R-85, S-214, T-33, U-14.

renewal, B-24, B-38, B-51, B-66, B-123, B-199, B-221,
B-223, C-71, C-98, C-157, C-245, C-316, C-332, D-96,
D-111, G-73, H-25, J-44, J-50, K-23, K-46, K-66,
K-77, L-22, L-28, L-36, L-63, L-77, M-13, M-95,
M-98, M-158, M-196, M-220, N-69, O-65, O-82, R-3, R-8,
R-32, R-52, R-83, S-20, S-122, S-169, S-208, U-12-13,
Y-10.

results of the Council, A-48, A-79, B-71, B-181, B-198,
B-218, C-10, C-30, C-67, C-75, C-83, C-129, C-240,
C-284, D-19, D-69, D-71, D-77, D-84, D-88, D-91,
E-40, E-49, F-24, F-36, F-49, F-57, G-1, G-65, H-78,
H-84, H-105, H-114, J-64, K-10, K-64, K-68, K-77, K-79,
L-59, L-103, M-5, M-26, M-102, M-143, O-7, O-52,
O-59, O-103, O-107, P-2, P-87, P-89, P-125, P-132,
P-137, R-2, R-8, R-23, R-53, R-90, S-8, S-12, S-36,
S-39, S-122, S-196, T-9, V-50, W-27, W-104, W-108,
Y-23.

reunion, see: ecumenism.

revelation, A-27, A-28, B-53-54, B-72, B-130, B-227,
C-174, C-184, C-217, C-273, D-34, D-103, D-118-119,
H-48, H-91, H-135, K-28, L-13, M-55, M-90, M-119, M-183a,
O-21, O-40, O-63, P-68, R-42, S-11, S-52, T-8, T-53,
U-14, W-70, W-91.

revolution, D-23, F-19, M-31, M-124, R-43.

Roman Synod, J-23.

Rumania, R-81.

Russian, see: Soviet Union.

Russian Orthodox, R-87, V-48, see also: Orthodox.

sacraments, M-21, M-51, O-19, R-34, W-10.

St. Augustine, H-130.

St. Francis, M-127.

St. Joseph, J-33.

St. Peter's Basilica, A-66, B-18, E-1, F-26, S-192.

St. Teresa, O-97.

schema 13, see: Church, modern.

Scotland, B-157.

secrecy, M-217.

secular institutes, H-29.

secular society, A-71, C-111, C-297, C-314, L-97, M-185,
    M-229, R-28, T-90.

seminaries, A-22, C-2, C-102, C-122, E-36, F-12, G-74,
    H-86, H-140, J-35, M-93, M-201, N-52, O-32, O-100,
    P-92, T-58, T-85.

senate, C-226, G-37.

service, B-217, see also: authority.

sex, B-125, C-92, C-172, P-36, see also: birth control.

Sheen, Fulton, M-36, S-93-95.

sisters, (as authors) A-60, C-172, D-10-13, D-91, F-66,
    J-65, K-23, L-95. M-101, M-103, M-116-119, P-49.

social justice, C-288, C-333, D-85, D-110, G-41, H-146,
    J-3, J-29, L-21, M-31, M-37, M-39, M-123, M-140.

Soviet Union, F-71, J-55, J-66, K-57, M-192-193, O-4,
    R-86, T-41, T-46, V-48.

Spain, A-63, C-73, D-93, S-163.

speeches, A-3, C-17, C-158, H-79, K-71, L-30, M-22, N-2, P-15-16, Y-20.

Suenens, Card. , C-42, S-205-211.

Switzerland, C-31, O-90.

Synod of bishops, P-85.

Syria, T-18.

Taize community, S-53.

Tardini, Card. , C-43.

television, see: press.

Tertiaries, T-4.

theology, A-5, A-9, A-41, B-24, B-49, B-224, C-164, F-76, L-31, L-61, M-10, M-57, M-168, M-188, M-222, M-232, N-62, N-74, O-48, P-1, P-20, R-10, S-36, S-92, S-157, T-6, V-43.

tradition, A-40, B-222, E-3, F-10, M-104, S-57, T-16, T-83.

Trent, Council, M-82, R-65.

truth, D-46, F-72, J-38-39, J-43, K-77, M-217, S-139, S-215, T-89, V-44.

Underground, The, C-284.

Unitarian, W-62.

United States, A-47, A-65, B-96, B-118-120, B-185, C-113, C-314, D-20, D-49, E-53, F-28, H-8-9, H-54, H-115, K-22, M-2, M-4, M-54, M-83, M-85, M-116, M-207, N-41, N-54, N-61-62, N-64, O-11, O-47, O-74, O-93, S-123, T-21, T-70, U-8, V-10, V-31, W-34, W-54, Y-5-8, Z-6.

Vatican I, B-93, C-193, C-220, K-20, M-82, M-156, U-11.

Vatican II (general), A-2, A-5, A-15, A-66, B-20, B-49,

Vatican II, 4th sess., A-20, A-24, A-50, A-76, B-31,
B-36, B-122, B-195, B-204, C-64, C-233, C-254, E-24,
F-29, F-63, G-52, H-111, H-125, I-8, I-15, J-6, L-12,
M-33, M-66, M-111, M-178, N-2, N-5, N-27, O-62,
O-77, P-10, P-14, P-28, P-55, R-96, S-32, S-82,
S-112, S-187, T-25, T-74, T-77, T-80, T-82, U-2,
V-37-39, V-41, V-57, W-3, W-45, W-84.

vernacular, B-215, C-312, G-63, V-53, see also: liturgy.

vespers, see: breviary.

Vischer, L., B-148, N-58, V-56-60.

vocations, E-36, N-20.

Wales, R-47.

war, B-139, C-108, C-206, D-102, E-35, F-31, O-10-11,
O-66, R-4-5, R-69, S-176-177, S-209, V-29, see also:
peace.

Waugh, E., B-10, C-69, C-198, W-14.

Wesley, John, C-26.

women, B-213-214, C-323, D-126, J-30, J-67, M-84,
S-161, T-87, V-10, W-73.

World Council of Churches, B-148, B-152, G-10, L-62,
L-65, N-40, N-47, O-88, P-88, S-113, V-6, V-56, V-60,
W-95-96.

World justice and development, M-6.

Wyszynski, Card., C-44-45.

Young Christian Workers, F-52-54, K-13.